Domain Driv[en] Design with Spring Boot

Dedicated to my grandmother. She was everything for me.

Author information

For any help please contact :
Amazon Author Page :
amazon.com/author/ajaykumar
Email : ajaycucek@gmail.com ,
ajaxreso@gmail.com
Linkedin :
https://www.linkedin.com/in/ajaycucek
Facebook :
https://www.facebook.com/ajaycucek
Youtube :
https://www.youtube.com/channel/UC1uXEe
btqCLYxVdzirKZGIA
Twitter : https://twitter.com/ajaycucek
Instagram :
https://www.instagram.com/ajaycucek/
Skype : ajaycucek

Table of contents

4

Module 1: Introduction

Getting Started

This book will explain how to apply domain-driven design concepts in a project with Spring Boot 2.0.6 and how to combine them with practices, such as unit testing (test driven development), relational databases and object relational mappers like JPA(Java Persistence API). We will see step by step how to grow an application from the very beginning to a full-fledged solution with DDD principles. Finally there will be two projects, one (static web project using jQuery & HTML) for user interface and another (Spring Boot + REST + JPA project) for API, logic and persistence.

- Entities
- Value objects
- Aggregates
- Repositories
- Bounded contexts
- Domain events

You will see the full process of building a software project using concepts such as entities, value objects, aggregates, repositories, bounded contexts, and domain events. In the way I will explain why we make one decision over another. You will learn what DDD concepts are applicable in which particular case and why it is so. We will see, how to apply the domain-driven design principles in a real world application.

Book Outline and Prerequisites

- **Introduction**
- **Starting with the First Bounded Context**
- **Introducing UI and Persistence Layers**
- **Extending the Bounded Context with Aggregates**
- **Introducing Repositories**
- **Introducing the Second Bounded Context**
- **Working with Domain Events**
- **Looking Forward to Further Enhancements**

The best way to learn how to apply the principles of domain-driven design is to actually go through the whole process of creating an application, and this is exactly what I am going to do. In the first module, we will talk about the core principles we will follow in this book. I will also give a quick overview of the basics of domain-driven design. You will see when the approach DDD proposes is applicable and why. I'll also introduce you to do the problem domain we'll be working in and show the UI of the application we'll be building throughout the book. In the next module, we'll start the development with some basic functionality. You will learn the differences between entities and value objects, which of them to use in your code base, and why. I'll also show the best practices for working with both concepts. In the third module, we'll discuss persistence and how to keep the domain model isolated, despite the requirements relational databases and object relational mappers impose. Next I'll show how we can combine the existing classes in aggregates. You will see how to find proper boundaries for aggregates and what trade-offs are there when it comes to defining an aggregate in your domain model. In module five, we'll talk about the repository pattern and how it correlates with aggregates. In the sixth module, we'll introduce the second bounded context and we'll discuss the guidelines behind the notion of bounded context itself. You will learn how bounded contexts relate to subdomains, how to find boundaries for them, and more. In the last module, we'll talk about domain events. We will implement domain events with the help of ApplicationEvent of Spring Boot. In the last module we will be looking forward to further enhancements. This book is going to be code heavy with a strong focus on the quality of the code. We will implement the project using the Java language and Spring Boot, so you will need at least some basic experience with java.

Area of Application for Domain-Driven Design

Most important attributes of every software project:
- Amount of data
- Performance
- Business logic complexity
- Technical complexity

Every good practice has its own limits. It's important to understand that domain-driven design is not a silver bullet, there are different kinds of projects and DDD is applicable to only a fraction of them. Let's elaborate on that. Every software project has a set of attributes, the most important of which are the amounts of data it operates, performance requirements, business logic complexity, and technical complexity. The amount of data the application works with may vary a lot in the modern days. Although most of the software we know works with data that can fit a single database instance, it is not necessarily the case for other types of projects. There are a lot of solutions that analyze and process huge amounts of row data, or in other words, big data. Performance requirements is another attribute that can differ for various types of projects. A simple utility, for example, often doesn't have much of them, as opposed to an online trading platform, which usually has a strict requirement to return any code with no more than tens of milliseconds timeframe. Business logic complexity are first to the degree to which the problem domain a software works in is complicated. For example, a CRUD application that performs basic create, read, update, delete operations doesn't carry a lot of complexity with it. At the same time, an ERP system, which automates a big chunk of the company's activity, must model all the processes the company acts upon and thus handle a lot of complex business roles. The business logic complexity of such a system may be extremely high. The last attribute I'd like to point out is technical complexity. You can think of it as a complexity of the algorithms you need to implement to make the software work. A good example here is low-level programming for embedded systems where you need to deal with many of the hardware systems manually. All right, so where do the domain-design practices fit in this picture? The techniques DDD proposes are useful if and only if the project you are working on has a lot of complex business rules. DDD won't help you if you work with big data, need to achieve outstanding performance, or program against hardware systems. The only purpose DDD concepts serve is to tackle business logic complexity.

DDD will not help in Twitter like applications because :

- **Business logic complexity : Low**
- **Amount of data   : High**
- **Performance   : High**

So, if you need to create a Twitter-like application, domain-driven design won't help you much with that, because the challenge in this type of software comes out not from its business roles. The business logic itself is pretty simple in Twitter. What makes it hard to implement is the great performance and scalability requirements.

DDD will help in Enterprise applications because :

- Amount of data   : Low
- Performance   : Low
- Business logic complexity : High
- Technical complexity   : Low

A typical example of software with complicated business logic is enterprise-level applications. It is true that most of enterprise projects don't have outstanding performance requirements, they operate moderate amounts of data, and developers working on them usually don't have to deal with technical complexity by their own, because there are plenty of tools that abstract out this kind of complexity for them. The biggest challenge in such projects is to handle business logic complexity in such a way that it would be possible to extend and maintain the solution in the long run. That is exactly the task that the domain-driven design practices are aimed to solve. They help us create code, which not only fully powers the problem, but also does it in the simplest, and thus the most maintainable way possible.

Why Domain-Driven Design?

Core principles in software development :

- YAGNI (you are not gonna need it)
- KISS (keep it short and simple)

Let's set some groundwork and talk about the basic principles we will follow in this book. In my opinion, there are two core principles in software development to which every programmer should adhere in most cases. They are YAGNI and KISS. YAGNI stands for you are not gonna need it, and basically means you should implement only the functionality you need in this particular moment. You shouldn't try to anticipate the future needs, because most of the functionality you develop just in case turns out to be unused and thus, just a waste of time. KISS stands for keep it short and simple. This principle is about making the implementation of the remaining functionality as simple as possible. The point here is that the simpler your code is, the more readable, and thus more maintainable it becomes. These principles are important, because they help solve two major problems we face when building software projects: shortening the time needed for development, and keeping the code base maintainable in the long run. The beauty of domain-driven design is that its practices complement these two software development principles. It allows us to extract the central part of the problem domain and simplify it, removing most of the necessary complexity. The ability to express business logic in the clearest way possible is a single trait that makes domain-driven design so appealing in enterprise-level applications. It is hard to estimate how important that is. The most difficult task in the modern business line software is to keep that complexity under control. There is only this much complexity we can deal with at a time. If the code exceeds it, it becomes really hard, and at some point, even impossible, to change anything in the software without introducing some unexpected side effects. Extending such a project becomes a pain and usually results in a lot of bugs. This, in turn, slows the development down and may eventually lead to failure of the project. Uncontrollable growth of complexity is one of the biggest reasons why software projects fail. Domain-driven design helps prevent it. You will see that in this book we'll make a continuous effort to keep our code base as simple and as expressive as possible.

Main Concepts of Domain-Driven Design

- Ubiquitous Language : Bridges the gap between developers and experts

Let's highlight the main concepts of domain-driven design. In this book, I assume you already know the theory behind DDD, so I'll keep the description short. The first one is the notion of ubiquitous language, that is, the language structured around the domain model and used by all team members to refer to the elements of that domain. You might have noticed that in many projects, domain experts and developers use different sets of terms when they talk about the domain. This difference leads to misunderstandings and slows the overall development process down. The notion of ubiquitous language helps eliminate the barrier. Domain-driven design suggests us to explicitly point those differences out and adjust the terminology to comply with a single ubiquitous language. Let's say, for example, that you have developed a sales system. In this system, you have a class called

Product, which is an atomic sale unit. Let's also say you also notice that the domain experts refer to this element as both Product and Package. In this case, you should call attention to this disparity and suggest to use a single term to avoid confusion. The concept of ubiquitous language also means you should keep your code base in sync with this single terminology and name all your classes and tables in the database after the terms in the ubiquitous language. All this helps bridge the gap and set the groundwork for efficient communication.

- Bounded Context: Clear boundaries between different parts of the system

Another important part of domain-driven design is the concept of bounded contexts. Often an application grows so much that it becomes hard to maintain its code base as a whole. Code elements that make sense in one part of the system may seem completely irrelevant in another. In this case, the best solution would be to separate these parts from each other explicitly. That is where this concept helps us. It allows us to clearly define the boundaries of these parts, hence the name bounded context.

Sales	Product	Support
	Attribute 1	
	Attribute 2	
	Attribute 3	

If your system consists of two parts, one of which is sales and the other is support, it would be a good decision to introduce a separate bounded context for each of them and explicitly state the relation between them. We will see how we can define bounded contexts in our code base in the future modules.

- Core domain : Focus on the most important part of the system

The third concept is the notion of core domain. Domain-driven design states that the main part of any system is its business logic, and not all, but the most intrinsic piece of it, that is, the problem the software is meant to solve is core domain. In the sales application example, there might be lots of business logic, but not all of it is essential. For instance, you might have a bookkeeping functionality that can be easily delegated to an external software. It is easy to do that, because it is not the core problem your application is built for, and it's cheaper to just buy an existing solution rather than trying to implement it from scratch. Domain-driven design proposes that we always focus most of our efforts on the core domain. These concepts, ubiquitous language, bounded context, and core domain, are the most important parts of domain-driven design. You can think of them as the strategic elements of DDD. The other notions, such as entities, value objects, and repositories, comprise the tactics of how you should build your software project.

Domain-Driven Design Is Not Only About Writing Code

| Developer | ⟷ | Domain Expert |

Domain-driven design is not only about writing code, though. Adhering to the DDD practices also implies a heavy communication process between developers and domain experts. It's important to have a direct access to the experts in your problem domain, because it's the only way to get the complete information about the problem you are solving. To get the most of domain-driven design, you should constantly refine your domain knowledge with the help of the experts in your company, and it shouldn't be a one-way process. If you see any inconsistencies in the language the experts use or in the model they draw, state it. It may be that you find a way to describe and solve the problem in a much simpler way that it was proposed in the beginning. Constantly work with the experts and strive to help them simplify or even completely rethink the problem. Your code, if built using the ubiquitous language, can become a great help for that. You may see some edge cases that weren't clear enough in the beginning, or you may find how to redefine the problem statement in a much cleaner and more concise manner. Another implication of domain-driven design is that you should always strive to become a domain expert yourself. Software developers are often enthusiastic about coding tasks that regard to building an infrastructure for the future project. Such tasks often seem interesting as they entail some technical challenge. Also, because of that technical nature, the knowledge acquired when solving them can be reused in other projects. All these make such activities compelling to many developers. Nevertheless, to benefit from the domain-driven design techniques the most, you should always try to dive into the domain you are working in as much as possible. This might seem boring at first, and may feel like a waste of time, because the domain knowledge you get working on one project can hardly be applied to another, but in the reality, it is not the case. First of all, if you obtain deep domain knowledge, it will help you do the best job that a programmer could possibly do. This knowledge will guide you through the code you write. It will help you look at it from the domain expert's point of view. This skill is indispensable, as it allows you to combine the best of the two worlds, write technically correct code on one hand, and express the domain knowledge with it on the other. Secondly, although problem domains are different from project to project, the skill of systematizing them with code is reusable. The more you learn the domain you work in, and the more you try to define it in your code base, the better you become at it. Eventually you will see patterns and will be able to work on new domains with ease, and it will also help you learn your domains more quickly.

Onion Architecture and Domain Isolation

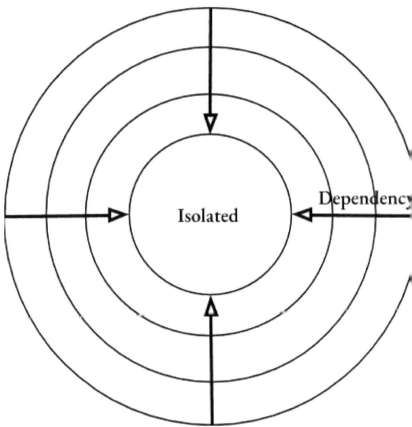

Let's look at the structure of a typical application built with the domain design principles in mind. DDD notions form a construction named onion architecture. It is called so because it resembles an onion with multiple layers and a core inside. Upper layers depend on the lower ones, but the lower layers don't know of the upper. It might seem similar to a classic onion layer architecture entities. The difference here is that onion architecture emphasized the fact that the core part of this structure cannot depend on anything else, except itself. It means that the core elements of our domain model should act in isolation from others. This is an important point. We will talk about it in a minute.

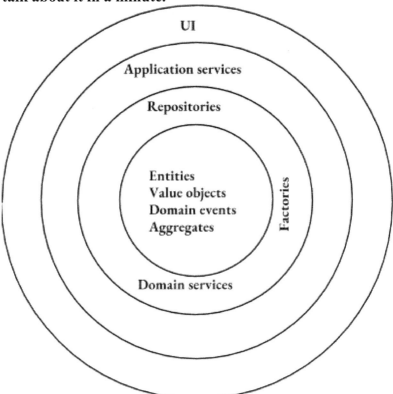

Let's place the building blocks of domain-driven design in this picture. The core part of this so-called onion is the notion of entity, value object, domain event, and aggregate. The next layer consists of repositories, factories, and domain services. Application services go beyond that, and finally, UI is the outermost layer, if, of course, the application contains a user interface. You might wonder where the database belongs in this picture. All work with a database should be encapsulated into repositories. They can refer to it either directly or use an ORM, but the general rule should remain. The code working with the data storage must be gathered under the repositories in your domain model. These four elements, entities, value objects, domain events, and aggregates, are the most basic. They can refer to each other, for example, and then they can contain a value object or a value object can keep a reference to an aggregate root, but they cannot work with other DDD notions, such as repositories and factories. Similarly, repositories, factories, and domain services can know of each other and the four basic elements, but they should not refer to the application services.

CORE DOMAIN :

Entity,   Domain Event,   Value Object ,   Aggregate

- **Domain knowledge**   :
  YES
- **Persistence logic**   :
  NO
- **Construction logic**   :
  NO
- **Mapping to the database logic**   :
  NO

So why is this kind of isolation is so important? Why should we keep the four core elements of the domain model separated from others? The main reason is the separation of concerns. Entities, value objects, domain events, and aggregates carry the most important part of the application, its business logic. They don't contain all of it, of course. Repositories and factories can keep some of the business logic as well, but these four elements do include most of it. In the situation where you have some elements so deeply involved in the problem domain representation, it is vital to keep them as free as possible from other duties. Hence, the notion of separation of concerns. I'd like to emphasize it once again. It is crucial to leave entities and value objects to do only one thing, represent the domain logic in your application. In practice, it means they shouldn't contain any knowledge about how they are persisted or how they are created. These two operations must be up to repositories and factories. They also shouldn't contain any knowledge about the tables and columns in the database where they are stored. This must be given away to data mappers. All they should know of is the domain they represent. Remember, the cleaner you keep your domain model, the easier it is to reason about it and to extend it later on. Inability to maintain proper separation of concerns in enterprise-level applications is one of the biggest reasons why code bases become a mess, which leads to delays and even failure of the project. It is not always possible to separate them completely, though, and there always will be some elements not related to your domain you cannot get rid of.

```
public class Product{
        public String name;
        public String getName(){
            return name;
        }
        protected Product(){}
        public Product(String name){
        name= name;
        }
}
```

An example here would be the necessity to create a parameter-less constructor in your entities to satisfy object-relational mappers. Nevertheless, it is possible to keep those elements under control so that they introduce almost no overhead to your domain clauses. Or we can create all together separate ProductDto class only for persistence of above Product class and this ProductDto class can also be used for data transfer to UI.

- Clean domain model
- Proper separation of concerns
- Dealing with ORM side effects

You will see how to do this in practice in the next modules, how to keep the domain model clean, how to maintain proper separation of concerns, and how to deal with the side effects object-relational mappers introduce.

Modeling Best Practices

- Focus on the Core Domain

If you follow DDD principles that the domain model becomes the heart of your software, this fact entails a guideline of how you should work with the applications code base. Focus on the core domain first, and pay most of your attention to it. In practice, it means that you should always start the development with modeling the core domain, even if you don't have any UI or database structure yet. Start experimenting with the model with the help of unit tests. User interface and the database are important elements of the system as well, of course, but the core domain is the part you should focus on the most. It might be hard to make such a shift, especially if you are used to building software starting from the database structure, but this shift is worth it. The investments in your domain model pay off greatly over time. It also means that in a typical enterprise application, any infrastructure code is less important than the core domain. Make sure you keep your business logic adherent and don't allow it to dissolve in the infrastructure code.

Domain-Driven Design and Unit Testing

When it comes to unit testing, it's important to keep a balance between the test coverage and the amount of effort you put into tests. 100% coverage is an expensive mark to reach, and it doesn't necessarily provide proportional value to the quality of your software. In most enterprise-level applications, the value distribution corresponds to the number of unit tests in this way. The closer we get 100%, the less value the additional tests provide us with. At the same time, the amount of effort we put in their creation grows linearly. It means that at some point, the value we get from the additional tests doesn't justify the resources we invest in them. At that point where we are better off to stop building up the coverage, as it wouldn't give us much besides a good-looking coverage number. The exact location of that point would differ from project to project, but the general trend remains. You should employ the same pragmatic principles in an application built with the domain-design principles in mind. In practice, it means you should cover with unit tests only those parts of your code base that are the most significant to the application, and this is the innermost layer in your onion architecture, entities, value objects, aggregates, and domain events, the elements which contain most of the domain knowledge of your application. It's a good idea to get 100% or close to 100% as coverage of them. That is another reason why we should keep the core layer of the domain model isolated from other parts of the application, such as database, email service, and so on. A good separation of concerns help create testable code, which doesn't require any mocks or other test doubles to be tested. If you find your unit test hidden in the database or some other external dependencies, it's a strong sign your domain model is not properly isolated. But what about the other parts of your code base? Shouldn't they be covered with tests as well? They definitely should, but it doesn't have to be unit tests. Moreover, we are better off not employing unit testing for those types of functionality, but rather use integration testing instead. That is, automated tests which cover several pieces of the application at once. Throughout this book, you will see this pragmatic approach to unit testing in practice. You will also see how easy it is to implement them due to great isolation we will achieve for our domain model.

The Problem Domain
Introduction

Now, let's talk about the problem domain
we'll be building our software for. We will
need to model the work of automated
machines. There will be two of them a snack
machine and an automated teller
machine (ATM). The principles I will be
describing are applicable to any kind of
enterprise-level applications. We will start
with snack machine. This is how its interface
will look like.

Chocolate price:$ Soda price:$ Gum price:$

Chocolate quantity: Soda quantity: Gum quantity:

| Buy a Chocolate | | Buy a Soda | | Buy a Gum |

Money inserted :$

| Insert 1 cent coin | | Insert 10 cent coin | | Insert 25 cent coin |

| Insert 1 dollar note | | Insert 5 dollar note | | Insert 20 dollar note |

| Return Money |

No of coins and notes in Snack machine :

No. of 1 cent coin :   No. of 10 cent coin :   No. of 25 cent coin :

No. of 1 dollar note :   No. of 5 dollar note :   No. of 20 dollar note :

This is the end result, but keep in mind that
we will come to this result interactively. Also,
our primary focus in this book is not the user
interface itself, so don't pay too much
attention to the visual presentation. Our task

is to model the snack machine so that it can sell snacks in exchange for cash. We won't pay attention to such details as how it recognized notes and coins or how the products are dispensed physically. What we are going to focus on is the actual business logic behind the device, what rules it should follow when dealing with taking money in, returning change, selling products, and so on. Snack machines will have three slots for snacks. One slot contains chocolates, 2nd slot contains cans of soda, and 3rd slot contains gums. In a real snack machine, there would be more different products of course, but we'll stick to only three in this book, just for the sake of brevity. The amount of money a user inserted in snack machine is displayed in the "Money inserted section". We can insert only 1 cent coins, 10 cent coins, 25 cent coins, 1 dollar notes, 5 dollar notes & 20 dollar notes. In this application, we assume there are no other coins or notes, just to make our task simple. In order to buy something, you need to insert a coin or a note and select which product you want to buy by pressing on one of these three buttons(Buy a Chocolate, Buy a Soda, Buy a Gum), so the overall process looks like this. I will insert in three $1 notes and press on "Buy a Chocolate" button. After that, the number of chocolates is decreased by one. We will reveal the details of the requirements as we start implementing the snack machine functionality. I hope you get the overall idea behind it. Another task we will have is modeling the work of an ATM.

Money inside :$
Money charged :$

Take Money

No of coins and notes in Atm :
No. of 1 cent coin :   No. of 10 cent coin :   No. of 25 cent coin :
No. of 1 dollar note :   No. of 5 dollar note :   No. of 20 dollar note :

Here a user can withdraw some cash from the bank account with a small fee. For example, I can enter one dollar in the textfield and press button "Take Money" and the number of $1 notes inside the ATM is decreased. Lastly here is head office .

Balance : $20.2
Cash : $2636

Snack machines	ATMs
Id Money 1 $0 2 $263.6	Id Cash 1 $1298 2 $527.2

Move cash from Snack machine to Head office :
Enter SnackMachine Id   Unload

Move cash from Head office to Atm :
Enter Atm Id   Load

And finally, we will need Head office to move the accumulated cash from ATMs to snack machines, and also keep a record of the

balance we have of all charges made by our ATMs. So this is the project we'll be working on in this book. I'll explain the design decisions we'll be making as we progress with our code, as well as common pitfalls developers usually run into when they start applying domain-driven design principles in practice. As we evolve our application, we will come up with different DDD notions gradually. I'll show how they fit the problem and how to choose between them, given particular circumstances.

Summary

- DDD area of application
- Core software design principles: YAGNI and KISS
- Main DDD concepts: ubiquitous language, bounded context and core domain
- DDD is not only about writing code
- Onion architecture and domain model isolation
- DDD and unit testing

In this module, you learned in what types of projects we should use the DDD principles. You also saw a quick overview of the software design principles, such as YAGNI, which stands for implementing only the functionality you need right now, and KISS, which proposes the use of the simplest solution possible. These two principles can help greatly as you go along with your project. The beauty of domain-driven design is that its principles perfectly align with this tool. DDD helps you break a problem into consumable chunks and reduce its complexity to a level where it's no longer hard to understand and implement. We'll look to the main DDD concepts: ubiquitous language, bounded context, and core domain. We talked about the importance of communication with domain experts, which needs to be two-sided, and the importance of the domain knowledge itself. We discussed the notion of onion architecture and why we should keep the domain model isolated. We also looked at the pragmatic approach to unit testing, which gives us the best return of investments. Alright, the development is about to start now. The best way to learn how to solve problems with DDD is to actually solve one, so be prepared to dive into the problem domain in this book and walk through it with me. I also recommend to re-read this module after we are done with the others, as you will be able to link the knowledge of the actual implementation with the groundwork we have set here.

Module 2: Starting with the First Bounded Context

Introduction

In this module, we will begin the actual development process. We'll start off with the basic functionality for our model of a snack machine, inserting coins and notes to the machine and returning the money. You will see how entities differ from value objects and learn the best practices for working with them.

Vocabulary Used

- Domain : The problem we are working on. The problem our software is going to solve.
- Terms "Domain " & "Problem domain" are synonymous.
- Core domain is a subset of "Problem domain" or "Domain"

- Domain Model : The solution for the problem. The artifact of the solution.
- Terms "Business logic", "Business rules", "Domain logic, "Domain knowledge" & "Domain model are synonymous

Before we start, let's take a minute to define the terms we'll be using in this book. You might have seen many of them in the past, but it's not always clear what they mean in different circumstances. First of all, I use the terms problem domain and domain interchangeably. They mean the actual problem our software is going to solve, the purpose it is built for. The term core domain is a subset of this, too. It is the essential part of the problem domain, the part which cannot be delegated to an external solution and must be resolved by us developers. Also, the terms business logic, business rules, domain logic, domain knowledge, and domain model are synonymous. You can think of them this way, the business logic you enclose in your code represents the knowledge that you as a software developer have about the problem domain. You express this knowledge by codifying a model of the domain you are working in, hence the term domain model. The business logic of an application typically resides in the two innermost layers of the onion architecture. I refer to the notions from these two layers as domain classes, so a domain class might be a repository, an entity, and so on, but not an application service. We will talk about the application services in the next module.

Problem Description

- **Insert money into the Machine**
- **Return the money back**
- **Buy a snack**

The first bounded context tool I will start with is snack machine. We will talk about the ways to represent bounded contexts later in this book. For now, we will focus on the machine model implementation. Our first task will be to model the way it works with coins and notes. So what are the operations we should be able to perform with money? Obviously we need a way to insert them into the machine. Also, if we change our mind, then we should be able to take the inserted money back. And finally, we may want to buy something. In this case, the amount of money we inserted should go to the machine permanently, and we should get back the change. We will take a shortcut in this module and implement a simplified version of the purchase functionality, and we will extend it in the future modules.

Starting with Snack Machine

We'll start the development with the core domain, the model of the snack machine. Here's the solution for our application. You can see there is only one project. In it, we will store our business logic, utilities, and data access code.

Create a Spring boot project as per below steps ;

Step 1: Open the link : https://start.spring.io/
Step 2: In front of Generate a, select "Gradle Project" and in front of With select "Java" with spring boot version as 2.0.6.
Step 3: Add group name as ddd and artifact name as logic.
Step 4: Add three dependencies as JPA, Rest Repositories and H2.
Step 5: Click on generate project and save it in your Eclipse workspace and import it as gradle project in Eclipse.
We will see the magic of spring boot in future modules.
We will see how to build and start this project in future modules.

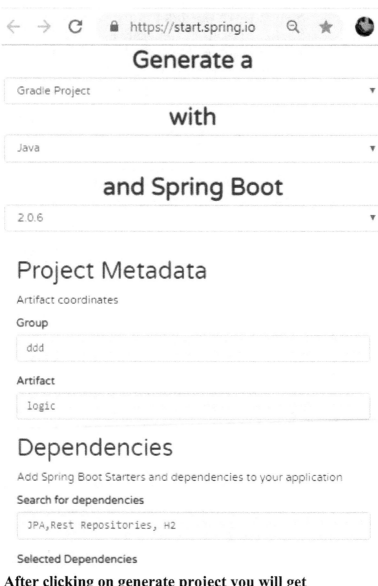

← → C 🔒 https://start.spring.io 🔍 ★ 🌑

Generate a

Gradle Project ▾

with

Java ▾

and Spring Boot

2.0.6 ▾

Project Metadata

Artifact coordinates

Group

ddd

Artifact

logic

Dependencies

Add Spring Boot Starters and dependencies to your application

Search for dependencies

JPA,Rest Repositories, H2

Selected Dependencies

**After clicking on generate project you will get
two classes LogicApplication.java and
LogicApplicationTests.java like this :
package ddd.logic;
import
org.springframework.boot.SpringApplication;**

34

```java
import
org.springframework.boot.autoconfigure.Spri
ngBootApplication;
@SpringBootApplication
public class LogicApplication {
    public static void main(String[] args) {
        SpringApplication.run(LogicApplica
tion.class, args);
    }
}
package ddd.logic;
import org.junit.Test;
import org.junit.runner.RunWith;
import
org.springframework.boot.test.context.Spring
BootTest;
import
org.springframework.test.context.junit4.Sprin
gRunner;
@RunWith(SpringRunner.class)
@SpringBootTest
public class LogicApplicationTests {
    @Test
    public void contextLoads() {
    }
}
```

You will get build.gradle file too :

```gradle
buildscript {
    ext {
        springBootVersion =
'2.0.6.RELEASE'
    }
    repositories {
        mavenCentral()
    }
    dependencies {
        classpath("org.springframework.boo
t:spring-boot-gradle-
plugin:${springBootVersion}")
```

```
        }
}
apply plugin: 'java'
apply plugin: 'eclipse'
apply plugin: 'org.springframework.boot'
apply plugin: 'io.spring.dependency-
management'
group = 'ddd'
version = '0.0.1-SNAPSHOT'
sourceCompatibility = 1.8
repositories {
     mavenCentral()
}
dependencies {
     implementation('org.springframework.bo
ot:spring-boot-starter-data-jpa')
     implementation('org.springframework.bo
ot:spring-boot-starter-data-rest')
     runtimeOnly('com.h2database:h2')
     testImplementation('org.springframewor
k.boot:spring-boot-starter-test')
}
Settings.gradle file.
setting.gradle:
rootProject.name = 'logic'
Add this below class to the project in the
package ddd.logic.:
package ddd.logic;
public final class SnackMachine {
     private int oneCentCount;
   private int tenCentCount ;
   private int quarterCount ;
   private int oneDollarCount ;
   private int fiveDollarCount;
   private int twentyDollarCount;

   public void insertMoney(int oneCentCount,

            int tenCentCount ,
```

```
            int quarterCount ,
            int oneDollarCount ,
            int fiveDollarCount,
            int twentyDollarCount) {
        oneCentCount += oneCentCount;
        tenCentCount += tenCentCount;
        quarterCount += quarterCount;
        oneDollarCount += oneDollarCount;
        fiveDollarCount += fiveDollarCount;
        twentyDollarCount +=
twentyDollarCount;
    }

    public void returnMoney() {

    }
}
```

This is the class for the SnackMachine, and note the use of the final keyword. It's a good practice to give your code as few privileges as possible by default. So, to insert money to the snack machine, we need to have a place where the coins and notes will be stored. The easiest way to do this is to introduce separate properties for each type of coin and note, so that we know exactly how many of them are in the machine right now. You can see in the above class a separate property for the number of one cent coins, quarters, and so on. The actual method, then, could look like shown above. We accept an amount of money, and just add them to the money we have in the machine. So far, so good. The second function our snack machine should have is the ability to return the money we inserted in case the user changed their mind. This raises a problem, as we don't distinguish the money the user inserted from the money that was in the machine beforehand, so it can't say how much money we should return to the user.

```java
package ddd.logic;
public final class SnackMachine {
    private int oneCentCount;
    private int tenCentCount ;
    private int quarterCount ;
    private int oneDollarCount ;
    private int fiveDollarCount;
    private int twentyDollarCount;

    private int oneCentCountInTransaction;
    private int tenCentCountInTransaction ;
    private int quarterCountInTransaction ;
    private int oneDollarCountInTransaction ;
    private int fiveDollarCountInTransaction;
    private int
twentyDollarCountInTransaction;

    public void insertMoney(int oneCentCount,

            int tenCentCount ,
            int quarterCount ,
            int oneDollarCount ,
            int fiveDollarCount,
            int twentyDollarCount) {
        oneCentCountInTransaction +=
oneCentCount;
        tenCentCountInTransaction +=
tenCentCount;
        quarterCountInTransaction +=
quarterCount;
        oneDollarCountInTransaction +=
oneDollarCount;
        fiveDollarCountInTransaction +=
fiveDollarCount;
        twentyDollarCountInTransaction +=
twentyDollarCount;
    }
```

```java
    public void returnMoney() {
        oneCentCountInTransaction = 0;
        tenCentCountInTransaction = 0 ;
        quarterCountInTransaction = 0 ;
        oneDollarCountInTransaction = 0 ;
        fiveDollarCountInTransaction = 0;
        twentyDollarCountInTransaction = 0;
    }

    public void buySnack() {
        oneCentCount +=
oneCentCountInTransaction;
        tenCentCount +=
tenCentCountInTransaction;
        quarterCount +=
quarterCountInTransaction;
        oneDollarCount +=
oneDollarCountInTransaction;
        fiveDollarCount +=
fiveDollarCountInTransaction;
        twentyDollarCount +=
twentyDollarCountInTransaction;

        oneCentCountInTransaction = 0;
        tenCentCountInTransaction = 0 ;
        quarterCountInTransaction = 0 ;
        oneDollarCountInTransaction = 0 ;
        fiveDollarCountInTransaction = 0;
        twentyDollarCountInTransaction = 0;
    }
}
```

The solution shown in previous page class, is to introduce a separate set of properties, which would define the amount of money that is currently in the transaction. This is the money the user will be able to get back or use to make a purchase. When the user inserts a coin or a note, this money is added to the money in transaction instead of the money that belongs to the machine, so we need to change the insertMoney method, like code in prevous page. The return method then just returns all the money that the user inserted. We can model this behavior by nullifying the corresponding properties. And finally, we should be able to buy a snack. For now, we can depict it like this. Just move all the money in transaction to the money inside the machine and nullify the transaction money after that. All right, let's overlook this implementation again in previous page . There is a concept here, which can be extracted out of the snack machine clause. I bet you already guessed that it's the notion of money. Indeed, we have two identical sets of properties. They represent the money the machine has, the amount of money inside, and the amount of money inserted by a user.

We can introduce an abstraction, a new class called Money, and now we are able to move all the money-related members to this class, and also add an addition operator to it. What this operator does is it introduces a plus function. It takes two money instances and creates a new one, which consists of all coins and notes from the original two. Now we are able to add just a single property, moneyInside, and remove all these properties from here. And another one for the money in transaction. The insertMoney method can also accept a money instance instead of the separate count parameters. Here we make use of the plus operator we introduced in the Money class. For the returnMoney method, we will also need to introduce some operation for clearing up the money instance to show that there is no longer any money in the transaction. We will talk about it later. For now, I'll just comment this line out. For the buySnack method, we are moving all the moneyInTransaction to the moneyInside, and also nullifying the instance. You can see here after we brought a new concept, money, the code of the snack machine, became much simpler. This is no coincidence. You will see that introducing a new abstraction often makes the overall solution easier to understand and maintain.

```
package ddd.logic;
public class Money{
    private int oneCentCount;
    private int tenCentCount ;
    private int quarterCount ;
    private int oneDollarCount ;
    private int fiveDollarCount;
    private int twentyDollarCount;

    public Money(int oneCentCount, int
tenCentCount, int quarterCount, int
oneDollarCount, int fiveDollarCount, int
twentyDollarCount){
    this.oneCentCount = oneCentCount;
    this.tenCentCount = tenCentCount;
    this.quarterCount = quarterCount;
    this.oneDollarCount = oneDollarCount;
    this.fiveDollarCount = fiveDollarCount;
    this.twentyDollarCount =
twentyDollarCount;
    }
    public static Money add(Money money1,
Money money2){
    Money sum = new Money(
            money1.oneCentCount +
money2.oneCentCount,
            money1.tenCentCount +
money2.tenCentCount,
```

```java
                money1.quarterCount +
money2.quarterCount,
                money1.oneDollarCount +
money2.oneDollarCount,
                money1.fiveDollarCount +
money2.fiveDollarCount,
                money1.twentyDollarCount +
money2.twentyDollarCount);
        return sum;
    }
}
public class SnackMachine {
    private Money moneyInside;
    private Money moneyInTransaction;

    public void insertMoney(Money money) {
        moneyInTransaction =
Money.add(moneyInTransaction, money);
    }

    public void returnMoney() {
        //moneyInTransaction = 0;
    }

    public void buySnack() {
        moneyInside =
Money.add(moneyInside,
moneyInTransaction);
        //moneyInTransaction = 0;
    }
}
```

Recap: Starting with Snack Machine

- **Start with the core domain**

42

- **Don't introduce several bounded contexts upfront**
- **Always look for hidden abstractions**

Let's recap what we came through in the previous demo. First of all, you saw we started with the core domain right away without modeling the UI or the database first. It's a good idea to always do this. You should always begin the project by experimenting with your domain model, as it's the most important part of your application. Secondly, always start with a single bounded context for all business logic in your application. Don't try to divide it into several pieces up front. While bounded contexts help reduce complexity of your code, the application is justified only when your code base is quite big already; otherwise, they won't reduce the complexity, but rather increase it instead. And thirdly, constantly evaluate your code and look for hidden abstractions. You saw that after we introduced the Money class, the code of the snack machine was simplified greatly. In our case, the presence of this abstraction was pretty adverse, of course, and it's not always possible to identify one in the most sophisticated situation. Nevertheless, if you see your code becomes awkward, you should test different approaches and examine if they fit your problem domain. It might be there is a hidden abstraction in your domain model that you didn't express just yet.

Entities vs. Value Objects

- **Snack Machine is Entity**

- **Money is Value Object**

At this point, we approached an important topic, the difference between entities and value objects. In our code base, we currently have two classes, Snack Machine and Money. They seem pretty similar to each other, but their semantics differ significantly. The Snack Machine class here is an entity, whereas money is a value object. Let's elaborate on that. The main difference between entities and value objects is in the way we identify them.

Types of Equality :

- **Reference equality**

```
+---------+    +---------+
|  Ref 1  |    |  Ref 2  |
+---------+    +---------+
         \        /
          \      /
+----------------------+
|    Object in Heap    |
+----------------------+
```

- **Identifier equality**

```
+-------------+    +-------------+
|  Object 1   |    |  Object 2   |
+-------------+    +-------------+
|   Id: 5     |    |   Id: 5     |
+-------------+    +-------------+
```

- **Structural equality**

```
+-------------+    +-------------+
|  Object 1   |    |  Object 2   |
+-------------+    +-------------+
| Name: "A"   |    | Name: "A"   |
+-------------+    +-------------+
| Country:"B" |    | Country:"B" |
+-------------+    +-------------+
```

There are three types of equality when it comes to comparing objects with each other. Reference equality, identifier equality, and structural equality. Reference equality means that two objects are deemed to be equal if they reference the same address in the memory. Identifier equality implies a class has an ID field. Two instances of such a class would be equal if they have the same identifiers. And finally, with structural equality, we can see there are two objects equal if all of their members match.

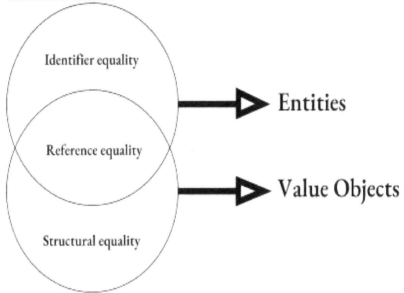

Entities :
- **Have inherent Identity**
- **Mutable**

Value Objects :
- **Don't have an Id field**
- **Can be treated interchangeably**
- **Immutable**

So how does the way we identify entities and value objects differ? The difference here is that identifier equality refers to entities exclusively, whereas value objects possess structural equality. In practice it means that value objects don't have an identifier field, and if two value objects have the same set of attributes, we can treat them interchangeably.

It makes a lot of sense if you look at the notion of money in our domain model. If we have two $1 notes, it doesn't really matter which of them we work with. We don't care about their identity. We can easily replace one set of coins and notes with another one, as long as these two sets have the same composition. At the same time, even if two snack machines have the same amount of money inside, we don't treat them interchangeably. We do care about which of them we work with. You can think of it in a similar way you would think of two people bearing the same name. We don't treat them as the same person because of that. They have their own inherent identity. Another distinction between the two notions is immutability. Value objects should be immutable in a sense that if we need to change such an object, we construct a new instance based on the existing object rather than changing it. On the contrary, entities are almost always mutable.

Lifespan :

Entity 1	Entity 2
Value Object 1	Value Object 1
Value Object 2	Value Object 2

The next difference is that value objects cannot live by their own. They should always belong to one or several entities. In our application, money doesn't make sense without a snack machine. If it does, the Money class would be an entity itself. We can put it another way. There always should be at least one entity that owns a value object. Again, in our case, it is the snack machine class, which contains two properties of the money type. An important implication from this point is that value objects don't have their own tables in the database. We will talk about it in more detail in the next module when we'll be discussion persistence for our domain model.

How to Recognize a Value Object in Your Domain Model?

It's not always clear if a concept in your domain model is an entity or a value object, and unfortunately, there are no objective attributes you could use to get to know it. Whether or not a notion is a value object fully depends on the problem domain. A concept can be an entity in one domain model and a value object in another. For example, in our system, the Money class is certainly a value object. At the same time, if you build a software for tracking the flow of the cash in the whole country, you do need to treat every single bill separately, as you need to gather statistics for each of them. In this case, the notion of money would be an entity, although you would probably name it note or a bill. Despite the lack of objective traits, you can still employ some techniques in order to attribute a concept to either entities or value objects. First of all, you should take into account the notion of identity we discussed previously. If you can safely replace an instance of a class with another one, which has the same set of attributes, that's a good sign this concept is a value object.

Structural Equality

Integers = Value Objects

```
public void method(){            public void
method(){
    int value1 = 5;                  Money
value1 = newMoney(5);
    int value2 = 5;                  Money
value2 = newMoney(5);
}                                }
```

A good way of thinking of value objects is comparing them to integers. Do you really care if the integer 5 is the same 5 that you used in the previous function? Definitely not. All 5s in the application are the same, regardless of how they were instantiated. That makes an integer essentially a value object. Now, ask yourself, is this notion in your domain looks like integer? If the answer is yes, then it's a value object. In our application, we don't really care where the instances of the Money class come from, and they are really similar to integers because of that. All said above has an important application.

Prefer value objects to entities :
- Value objects are light-weight
- Put most of business logic to value objects
- Entities act as wrappers

Always prefer value objects to entities. Value objects are immutable and more lightweight than entities. Because of that, they are extremely easy to work with. Ideally you should always try to put most of the business logic into value objects. Entities in this situation would act as wrappers upon them and provide more high level instructions. Also, it might be that a concept you saw as an entity at first essentially is a value object. For example, an address class in your system could be introduced as an entity initially. It may have its own ID field and a separate table in the database, but after visiting it, you might notice that in your domain, addresses don't actually have their own identity and can be used interchangeably. In this case, don't hesitate to re-factor your domain model and convert the entity into a value object.

Entity Base Class

A typical application contains a lot of entities, so there should be a base class where you can gather common behaviors for each of them. Let's discuss different approaches for creating such a base class.
public interface IEntity{ }
The first option we have here is to introduce an interface, like this. That way we'll be sure all domain entities in our model have some minimal functionality, the ID property. Although it might seem a good decision, in most cases, having an interface as a base entity is a bad idea.

- Doesn't show proper relations between entities

Use of an interface doesn't show the appropriate relationship between domain entities. Implementing an interface means that your class makes a promise to have some functionality defined in the interface.

- "Can-do" relationship :

```
public interface IEntity{ }
public class Entity1 implements
IEntity{ }
public class Entity2 implements
IEntity{ }
```

- "Is-a" relationship :

```
public abstract class Entity{ }
public class Entity1 extends
Entity{ }
public class Entity2 extends
Entity{ }
```

Two classes implementing the same interface don't tell us anything about their relationship. They can be related, but it also can be that they belong to entirely unconnected hierarchies. In other words, the IEntity interface introduces a can-do relationship, whereas domain entities should be connected to the base class by an is-a relation. Not only such classes should have common functionality, but they themselves are entities. The only way for us to avoid these drawbacks is to introduce an abstract base class.

```
package ddd.logic;
public abstract class Entity {
    protected long id;
    @Override
    public boolean equals(Object obj) {
        Entity other = (Entity) obj;
        if (other == null)
            return false;
        if (this == other)  // Reference
equality
            return true;
```

```java
        if
(!this.getClass().equals(other.getClass()))
            return false;
        if (this.id == 0 || other.getId() == 0)
            return false;
        return this.id == other.getId();
//identifier equality
    }
    @Override
    public int hashCode() {
        final int prime = 31;
        int result = 1;
        result = prime * result + (int) (id ^
(id >>> 32));
        return result;
    }
    public long getId() {
        return id;
    }
    protected void setId(long id) {
        this.id = id;
    }
}
```

Here is the actual code for the entity base class. As we discussed earlier, entities have their own inherent identity. The best way to represent this identity is to introduce a separate member, the ID property. It's a good idea to use a long type for this purpose by default, as such IDs are easier to work with than, say, GUIDs. The equals method is defined in the base object class and is often used internally. For example, when we call the contains method on the list of entities, jvm compares the objects inside the list with the target one by calling the equals method. The default equals implementation gives us only reference equality. As we discussed earlier, entities also possess the identifier equality, so we need to override this method in order to introduce it. Here's how it looks like inside. We try to cast the other object to Entity, compare the two references to each other, that gives us the reference equality. If the type of the entities is not the same, they cannot be equal no matter what IDs they have. Also, if any of the identifiers are 0, it means that the ID was not yet set with the entity, and we cannot compare it to other entities, because its identity is not yet established. And finally, if all previous checks are passed, we compare the identifiers themselves, which gives us identifier equality. Finally, we also need to implement the hashCode method. It's important for two objects which are equal to each other to always generate the same hash code.

```
public final class  SnackMachine extends
Entity {
     private Money moneyInside;
     private Money moneyInTransaction;

  public void insertMoney(Money money) {
       moneyInTransaction =
Money.add(moneyInTransaction, money);
  }

  public void returnMoney() {
       //moneyInTransaction = 0;
  }

  public void buySnack() {
       moneyInside =
Money.add(moneyInside,
moneyInTransaction);
       //moneyInTransaction = 0;
  }
}
```

Now, as we have the Entity base class, we can inherit our snack machine from it. This is our first fully-fledged entity shown above.

You saw the Entity base class we'll be using in our application.

Entity base class :
- Id property
- Equality members

It's important to remember that unlike value objects, each entity has their own identity. The best way to introduce this identity is to put it into the base class. The additional benefit here is that we are able to implement all required equality members in a single place. All entities in our domain model get them for free just by inheriting from the base class.

Value Object Base Class

Value Object base class :
- Don't have an Id property
- Can't place equality members to the base class

Value objects don't have their own identity, and thus they shouldn't have the ID property like entities. It also means that we cannot place all code required for equality in the base class. In order to implement structural equality, we need to know the internals of each value object class. Nevertheless, we can still gather some logic common to such classes.

```
package ddd.logic;
public abstract class ValueObject<T> {
    @Override
    public boolean equals(Object obj) {
        T valueObject = (T) obj;
```

```java
        if (valueObject == null)
            return false;
        return equalsCore(valueObject);
    }
    @Override
    public int hashCode() {
        return getHashCodeCore();
    }
    protected abstract boolean equalsCore(T
other);
    protected abstract int
getHashCodeCore();
}
```

Here's the code of the value object base class. You can see that we do override the Equals method, but delegate the actual work to the abstract equalsCore method, and the same is for getHashCode. We could just leave the equals and getHashCode methods without overriding them here, but this practice has two advantages. First, the new two methods are abstract, meaning that we won't forget to implement them in a derived value object class. The compiler will notify us about that. Second, we are making sure that the object common to the equalsCore method is of the same type as the current valueObject and it is not null. Thus, we don't need to duplicate these checks in the derived classes, we can just gather them here. Now let's look at how we can use this class.

```java
public class Money extends
ValueObject<Money>{
    private int oneCentCount;
    private int tenCentCount ;
    private int quarterCount ;
    private int oneDollarCount ;
    private int fiveDollarCount;
    private int twentyDollarCount;
```

```java
    public Money(int oneCentCount, int
tenCentCount, int quarterCount, int
oneDollarCount, int fiveDollarCount, int
twentyDollarCount){
        this.oneCentCount = oneCentCount;
        this.tenCentCount = tenCentCount;
        this.quarterCount = quarterCount;
        this.oneDollarCount = oneDollarCount;
        this.fiveDollarCount = fiveDollarCount;
        this.twentyDollarCount =
twentyDollarCount;
    }
    public static Money add(Money money1,
Money money2){
        Money sum = new Money(
                money1.oneCentCount +
money2.oneCentCount,
                money1.tenCentCount +
money2.tenCentCount,
                money1.quarterCount +
money2.quarterCount,
                money1.oneDollarCount +
money2.oneDollarCount,
                money1.fiveDollarCount +
money2.fiveDollarCount,
                money1.twentyDollarCount +
money2.twentyDollarCount);
        return sum;
    }
    @Override
    protected  boolean equalsCore(Money
other){
        return oneCentCount ==
other.oneCentCount
        && tenCentCount ==
other.tenCentCount
        && quarterCount ==
other.quarterCount
```

```
                    && oneDollarCount ==
other.oneDollarCount
            && fiveDollarCount ==
other.fiveDollarCount
            && twentyDollarCount ==
other.twentyDollarCount;
    }
    @Override
    protected int getHashCodeCore(){
        int hashCode = oneCentCount;
        hashCode = (hashCode * 397) ^
tenCentCount;
        hashCode = (hashCode * 397) ^
quarterCount;
        hashCode = (hashCode * 397) ^
oneDollarCount;
        hashCode = (hashCode * 397) ^
fiveDollarCount;
        hashCode = (hashCode * 397) ^
twentyDollarCount;
        return hashCode;
    }
}
```

We can derive money from it, and you can see
as soon as we introduced the inheritance, the
compiler tells us that we need to implement
the two abstract methods. So let's do that. For
the equalsCore method, we need to check the
equality for each of the properties. And the
same goes for the getHashCode method. All
members of the value object should take part
in the HashCode generation.

Entity base class	Value Object base class

Alright, let's reiterate it once again. The most
important distinction between entities and
value objects is the difference in the way we
identify them. There are three types of

equality. Reference equality belongs to both entities and value objects. Identifier equality to entities, structural equality to value objects. This means that each entity should have their own identity, which is best expressed using a separate ID property. It also means that we can create a single equality method that would feed every entity. Value objects at the same time don't have an identity, so they cannot have a separate ID field. The structural equality means that we need to implement the comparison logic in each value object class apart, but this task can be alleviated by factoring some common logic out to the base class.

When to Write Unit Tests

In the previous module, we talked about unit testing in the context of DDD. We discussed that we should cover with unit tests only the innermost layer of the onion architecture, entities, value objects, aggregates, and domain events. Now let's talk about when we should write unit tests. The process of test-driven development proposes that we employ the test-first approach. While it's true that DDD has a lot of benefits, in my opinion both test-first and code-first approaches are applicable in different circumstances.

Test-First	Code-First

In short, there are basically two modes in which we write code. With the first one, we are pretty sure what we want the code to do, so we can create unit tests up front before we actually start implementing the required functionality. On the other hand, we might be exploring new areas in our domain model. When experimenting with different ideas in code, we are not exactly sure how the implementation should look like. In this case, we are better off not trying to come up with unit tests up front and just try the code without them. The reason is that while experimenting, we often rewrite our code and even throw it away completely, and unit tests would only slow us down with that. If so, that we wrote the first draft of our domain model without any tests. We were experimenting with code and that resulted in a new concept, the Money class emerged. And now as we are finished with the experiments, we are pretty sure about how the code should look like. It is time now to enter the test-first mode and continue the development adherent to the DDD process.

Implementing the Money Class

Can we create a money instance with no value or with a negative one? The empty money instance does make sense in our domain model. After all, the snack machine we are modeling can have no money inside at some point. On the other hand, a negative value doesn't make sense and should be prohibited.

```
package ddd.logic;
public class Money extends
ValueObject<Money>{
    private int oneCentCount;
```

```java
private int tenCentCount ;
private int quarterCount ;
private int oneDollarCount ;
private int fiveDollarCount;
private int twentyDollarCount;

public Money(int oneCentCount, int
tenCentCount, int quarterCount, int
oneDollarCount, int fiveDollarCount, int
twentyDollarCount){
        if (oneCentCount < 0)
        throw new IllegalStateException();
    if (tenCentCount < 0)
        throw new IllegalStateException();
    if (quarterCount < 0)
        throw new IllegalStateException();
    if (oneDollarCount < 0)
        throw new IllegalStateException();
    if (fiveDollarCount < 0)
        throw new IllegalStateException();
    if (twentyDollarCount < 0)
        throw new IllegalStateException();

        this.oneCentCount = oneCentCount;
    this.tenCentCount = tenCentCount;
    this.quarterCount = quarterCount;
    this.oneDollarCount = oneDollarCount;
    this.fiveDollarCount = fiveDollarCount;
    this.twentyDollarCount =
twentyDollarCount;
    }
    public static Money add(Money money1,
Money money2){
        // same as above money class
    }
    @Override
    protected  boolean equalsCore(Money
other){
        // same as above money class
```

```
    }
    @Override
    protected int getHashCodeCore(){
        // same as above money class
    }
}
```
If oneCentCount is less than 0, then we should throw an invalid exception. And we need to replicate this validation for all parameters.

Building up the Money Class

At this point, it is pretty clear we will need at least two more methods from our Money class. Obviously, we will need to get the value a money instance represents so that we are not forced to calculate it manually all the time. Also, it is logical to have a subtraction operation along with the addition one, so we need to implement it as well. I need to make an important warning here. Always follow the YAGNI principle and refrain from adding any functionality up front. Remember, this principle is one of the most important, and you should always adhere to it when developing software projects. It might seem that by adding these two features to the Money class, we are violating this principle, because they are not used anywhere in our domain model yet. But I'm taking a shortcut here. I know that we will need them in the near future, because I already went through the development of this application. In a real world situation, you should always try not to introduce any code until you see that you cannot solve the task we are working on without it. the use cases expects the value to be non zero, but received 0 instead. The actual implementation is pretty simple.

```java
public class Money extends ValueObject<Money>{
    private int oneCentCount;
    private int tenCentCount ;
    private int quarterCount ;
    private int oneDollarCount ;
    private int fiveDollarCount;
    private int twentyDollarCount;

    private float amount ;
public float getAmount() {
        return  oneCentCount * 0.01f +
tenCentCount * 0.10f + quarterCount * 0.25f
+ oneDollarCount * 1f
                    + fiveDollarCount * 5f +
twentyDollarCount * 20f;
    }

    public Money(int oneCentCount, int
tenCentCount, int quarterCount, int
oneDollarCount, int fiveDollarCount, int
twentyDollarCount){
        // same as above money class
    }
    public static Money add(Money money1,
Money money2){
        // same as above money class
    }
    @Override
    protected  boolean equalsCore(Money
other){
        // same as above money class
    }
    @Override
    protected int getHashCodeCore(){
        // same as above money class
```

```
        }
}
```
We just need to sum up all the coins and notes
the money instance has, taking into account
their delimitation. It's a good time to make
some refactoring for our code at this point.
You can see the properties of the Money class
have public setters, which means that they can
be easily changed by the external code.
Remember, one of the attributes of value
objects is that they should be immutable. To
implement immutability, we could just hide
the properties from the outside world by
making them private, like this. To implement
a read-only property, I just need to remove
the setter, and here we are, our class is now
completely immutable.

```
public class Money extends
ValueObject<Money>{
        private int oneCentCount;
        private int tenCentCount ;
        private int quarterCount ;
        private int oneDollarCount ;
        private int fiveDollarCount;
        private int twentyDollarCount;

        private float amount ;
public float getAmount() {
        return  oneCentCount * 0.01f +
tenCentCount * 0.10f + quarterCount * 0.25f
+ oneDollarCount * 1f
                + fiveDollarCount * 5f +
twentyDollarCount * 20f;
        }

        public int getQuarterCount() {
                return quarterCount;
        }
        public int getOneCentCount() {
```

```
            return oneCentCount;
        }
        public int getTenCentCount() {
            return tenCentCount;
        }
        public int getOneDollarCount() {
            return oneDollarCount;
        }
        public int getFiveDollarCount() {
            return fiveDollarCount;
        }
        public int getTwentyDollarCount() {
            return twentyDollarCount;
        }
        public float getAmount() {
            return amount;
        }
// same as above money class
}
```

We need to do here is we need to take two instances and subtract one from the other. The resulting money instance should have the correct counts for each property. An important edge situation in this case is that we can try to subtract more than we have, so we need to make sure we prohibit such separations as well.

```
package ddd.logic;
public class Money extends
ValueObject<Money>{
    // all other codes are same as above
money class

    public Money substract(Money other){
        return new Money(
          oneCentCount - other.oneCentCount,
            tenCentCount -
other.tenCentCount,
```

```java
                quarterCount -
other.quarterCount,
                oneDollarCount -
other.oneDollarCount,
                fiveDollarCount -
other.fiveDollarCount,
                twentyDollarCount -
other.twentyDollarCount);
    }
    public Money add(Money other){
    Money sum = new Money(
        oneCentCount + other.oneCentCount,
        tenCentCount + other.tenCentCount,
        quarterCount + other.quarterCount,
        oneDollarCount +
other.oneDollarCount,
        fiveDollarCount +
other.fiveDollarCount,
        twentyDollarCount +
other.twentyDollarCount);
        return sum;
    }
}
```

Implementing the Snack Machine Class

Let's start implementing the snack machine
with the simplest method, returnMoney,
creating another file, SnackMachineTests in
src/test/java folder.

```java
package ddd.logic;
import org.junit.Test;
import ddd.logic.SnackMachine;
public class SnackMachineTest {
    @Test
```

```java
    public void
return_money_empties_money_in_transaction
(){
        SnackMachine snackMachine = new
SnackMachine();
    snackMachine.insertMoney(Dollar);
    snackMachine.returnMoney();

assertEquals(snackMachine.getMoneyInTrans
action().getAmount(), 0, 0);
    }
}
```

I create a SnackMachine here and insert a
dollar inside. And you can see, the test doesn't
like what we've done here so far. Insert
method throws a null pointer exception. The
problem is that we are trying to use the
moneyInTransaction instance without
initializing it. That's one of the benefits
continues test running provides us. We get the
feedback very quickly.

```java
public final class SnackMachine extends
Entity {
    private Money moneyInside;
    private Money moneyInTransaction;

    public void insertMoney(Money money) {
        moneyInTransaction =
Money.add(moneyInTransaction, money);
    }

    public void returnMoney() {
        //moneyInTransaction = 0;
    }

    public void buySnack() {
        moneyInside =
Money.add(moneyInside,
moneyInTransaction);
```

```
        //moneyInTransaction = 0;
    }
}
```

All right, so let's add a constructor, assign an empty instance to the moneyInside, and the same for the moneyInTransaction. The tests went green again.

```
public final class SnackMachine extends
Entity {
    private Money moneyInside;
    private Money moneyInTransaction;

    public SnackMachine() {
        moneyInside = new
Money(0,0,0,0,0,0);
        moneyInTransaction = new
Money(0,0,0,0,0,0);
    }

    public void insertMoney(Money money) {
        moneyInTransaction =
Money.add(moneyInTransaction, money);
    }

    public void returnMoney() {
        //moneyInTransaction = 0;
    }

    public void buySnack() {
        moneyInside =
Money.add(moneyInside,
moneyInTransaction);
        //moneyInTransaction = 0;
    }
}
```

Calling the returnMoney method, and verifying the amount of moneyInTransaction is 0. The test fails, and now we need to implement the method itself. Here we need to somehow clear the money that is currently in transaction. The first option that could come to mind is to introduce a clearer method and call it here, like this.

moneyInTransaction.clear();

This solution is not the best one, as it violates the immutability of the Money class. In order to implement such a method, we would need to change the state of the existing money instance. A better way of dealing with it is to just overwrite the instance with a new one, like this. This way we are keeping the money value object immutable.

```
public final class SnackMachine extends Entity {
    // all other codes are same as above

    public void returnMoney() {
        moneyInTransaction = new Money(0,0,0,0,0,0);
    }
}
```

You can see the tests are passing, so now we can do a bit of refactoring. First of all, creating a money instance and passing all six parameters to it all the time is a bit annoying. As our Money class is a value object, it's a good idea to create a static read-only field for the empty money instance. Here it is. Now we can replace the constructor with this field. And it turns out we can create a field for each coin and note as well. Cent, 10 cent, quarter, and so on. This enables us to simplify our test like this. Static using statements allow us to import a separate class and use its static members without specifying the class name. So, Money.Dollar here turns to just Dollar. And we can do the same in the snackMachine class. I can just assign the money instances the initial values and remove the constructor.

```java
public class Money extends
ValueObject<Money> {
    public static Money None = new
Money(0, 0, 0, 0, 0, 0);
    public static Money Cent = new Money(1,
0, 0, 0, 0, 0);
    public static Money TenCent = new
Money(0, 1, 0, 0, 0, 0);
    public static Money Quarter = new
Money(0, 0, 1, 0, 0, 0);
    public static Money Dollar = new
Money(0, 0, 0, 1, 0, 0);
    public static Money FiveDollar = new
Money(0, 0, 0, 0, 1, 0);
    public static Money TwentyDollar = new
Money(0, 0, 0, 0, 0, 1);
// rest codes are same
}
package ddd.logic;
import static ddd.logic.Money.None;
public final class SnackMachine extends
Entity {
    private Money moneyInside = None;
    private Money moneyInTransaction=
None;

  public void insertMoney(Money money) {
        moneyInTransaction =
Money.add(moneyInTransaction, money);
  }

  public void returnMoney() {
        moneyInTransaction = None;
  }

  public void buySnack() {
```

```
        moneyInside =
Money.add(moneyInside,
moneyInTransaction);
        //moneyInTransaction = 0;
    }
}
```
All right, another method we are going to cover with tests is the insertMoney method.
```
    @Test
    public void
inserted_money_goes_to_money_in_transactio
n() {
            SnackMachine snackMachine = new
SnackMachine();
        snackMachine.insertMoney(Cent);
        snackMachine.insertMoney(Dollar);

assertEquals(snackMachine.getMoneyInTrans
action().getAmount(), 1.01, 0);
    }
```
Create a new SnackMachine, insert in a Cent and a Dollar, and checking the amount of money is correct. The test passes, because we already implemented this functionality. At this point, we need to once again think of possible edge cases. Is it possible to insert not a single coin or note, but several of them all at once? That is probably a question we need to ask the domain expert, because at this point it's not obvious if the model we are building should support such a use case. And remember, communication between the developers and domain experts is vital and the domain during design practices put a great emphasis on this part of the development process. Let's say that we together with domain experts decided our domain should only accept a single coin or bill at a time. That makes sense, because that's

how a real snack machine's receiver works. So we need to add another test to verify that.

```java
@Test(expected = IllegalStateException.class)
  public void
cannot_insert_more_than_one_coin_or_note_
at_a_time() {
        SnackMachine snackMachine = new
SnackMachine();
        Money twoCent = Money.add(Cent,
Cent);
     snackMachine.insertMoney(twoCent);
  }
```

In the test, we need to create a twoCent money instance and try to insert it to the machine. The test would pass if the machine throws an exception. All right, to implement this, we need to specify all possible values we accept in the Insert method and check if the incoming instance is one of them.

```java
package ddd.logic;
import static ddd.logic.Money.None;
import java.util.Arrays;
public final class SnackMachine extends
Entity {
    private Money moneyInside = None;
    private Money moneyInTransaction=
None;

  public void insertMoney(Money money) {
        Money[] coinsAndNotes = {
Money.Cent, Money.TenCent,
Money.Quarter, Money.Dollar,
Money.FiveDollar,
                Money.TwentyDollar };
        if
(!Arrays.asList(coinsAndNotes).contains(mon
ey))
            throw new
IllegalStateException();
```

```
        moneyInTransaction =
Money.add(moneyInTransaction, money);
   }

   public void returnMoney() {
        moneyInTransaction = None;
   }

   public void buySnack() {
        moneyInside =
Money.add(moneyInside,
moneyInTransaction);
        //moneyInTransaction = 0;
   }
}
```
And finally, we need to finish the buySnack method.
```
@Test
     public void
money_in_transaction_goes_to_money_inside
_after_purchase() {
          SnackMachine snackMachine = new
SnackMachine();
     snackMachine.insertMoney(Dollar);
     snackMachine.insertMoney(Dollar);
     snackMachine.buySnack();

assertEquals(snackMachine.getMoneyInTrans
action(), None);

assertEquals(snackMachine.getMoneyInside()
.getAmount(), 2, 0);
   }
```
Here we are inserting two dollars to our machine, call in the buySnack method, and check the moneyInTransaction is empty, and the moneyInside contains two dollars after that. The implementation is pretty simple. We

just need to assign the moneyInside instance an empty value here.

```
public final class SnackMachine extends
Entity {
    // all other codes are same as above class

  public void buySnack() {
      moneyInside =
Money.add(moneyInside,
moneyInTransaction);
        moneyInTransaction = None;
  }
}
```

We are done with the first draft of the snack machine. It obviously lacks some significant parts. For example, the buy method should definitely deal with snacks somehow and not just take all inserted money. We will address this in the later modules when we'll be discussing aggregates and repositories. Also in the real world application, you would probably want to write more unit tests. For example, it's a good idea to check that a newly created snack machine doesn't contain any money in it. But I'll leave it aside just to keep our development process less verbose.

Recap: Implementing Money and Snack Machine

Previously, you saw how we implemented our first version of the Money and SnackMachine classes. A note that we kept the money value object immutable. Whenever we needed to perform such operations as addition or subtraction, we created a new instance of the class without changing the existing ones. The SnackMachine entity, on the other hand, is mutable. Mutability is an inherent trait for all entities. They change their state throughout the lifetime while maintaining immutable and unique identity. Also note that the SnackMachine entity contains not as much logic comparing to the money value object. All it does at this point is delegates most of its operations to the Money class. This is another good practice I mentioned earlier. Always try to delegate as much logic as possible from entities to value objects. Value objects are easy to maintain because of their immutability. During this phase of development, we stuck to the TDD process, meaning that we wrote the tests first, and then implemented the required functionality according to those tests. I intentionally demonstrated the whole process to show you how nicely domain-driven design can be combined with test-driven development. In the next modules, however, I will depart from adhering to the test-first approach just to speed our development up. But keep in mind that it's a good practice to follow this simple rule: write the code first when you're experimenting with your model and switch to the test-first mode when you have a good picture of how the code should look like. And, of course, while the test-driven development practices can be beneficial, you don't have to follow them in order to do domain-driven design, but remember to always cover your domain model with unit tests regardless of when you prefer to write them.

- Code-first approach for experiments
- Test-first approach after the experiments

- Always cover the model with unit tests

Summary

- Start off by working on the core domain
- Begin with a single bounded context
- Constantly search for hidden abstractions
- 3 distinctions between Entities and Value Objects
  - Reference vs structural equality
  - Mutability vs immutability
  - Lifespan: Value Objects should belong to Entities
- Compare Value Object to Integers
- Move logic from Entities to Value Objects
- TDD and DDD

In this module, we started the development with the first bounded context, which is snack machines. We focused on entities and value objects. You learned the differences and best practices behind these two notions. Let's reiterate through the most important moments of this module. First of all, try to begin the development by working with the core domain first. Your core domain, along with the unit tests covering it, is the most important part of the application you are building. Secondly, always start the development with a single bounded context. There is little value in dividing your application into several pieces up front, as you usually don't have enough information to make a competent decision about the proper boundaries at this point. Constantly evaluate your code and look for hidden abstractions in it. If you see your code becomes unclear or convey its meaning vaguely, it's a strong sign you missed an important abstraction. There are three main distinctions between value objects and entities. The first one refers to the way we identify them. There are three types of equality when it comes to comparing objects to each other. Entities possess identifier equality, meaning that we treat two entities as being the same only when they have the same identifier. Value objects, on the other hand, have structural equality. We can see there are two value objects to be equal if all their fields are the same. Value objects cannot have an identifier. The second distinction is that value objects are immutable data structures, whereas entities change during their lifetime. And finally, value objects cannot live by their own. They should always belong to an entity. In our application, for example, the money value object doesn't make sense without a snack machine. A snack machine composes too many instances. It also means that value objects shouldn't have their own tables in the database. We will elaborate on that topic in the next module. We discussed the techniques for recognizing a value object in the domain model. A good approach here is to compare one to an integer. If they have essentially the same semantics, you can be sure the class you are looking at is a value object. We also talked about an important practice of moving as much logic to value objects as possible. Value objects are lightweight and therefore are extremely easy to maintain and reason about. We looked at the code of the base entity and value object classes, and also saw why we cannot use .NET value types to create value objects. We discussed test-driven development in the context of domain-driven design and two approaches to write in unit tests. We will talk more about unit testing in the following modules. All right, we've made good progress here. In the next module, we will see how to introduce user interface and a database in the way that helps keep our domain model clean and isolated.

Module 3: Introducing UI and Persistence Layers

Introduction

In this module, we will talk about the user interface and the database for our domain model. We will see how they feed the application built with the domain-driven design principles in mind, and how to work with the object-relational mapper in a way that allows us to keep our domain model simple and clean.

Application Services and UI in the Onion Architecture

In our client layer, we will adhere to the MVC design pattern. MVC is not the primary focus of this book, so I'll keep the descriptions short, just to give you an idea where it belongs in the context of the onion architecture we discussed in the first module. MVC stands for Model View Controller. The Model part here is the domain model we discussed previously. The View is the UI layer in our application, and the Controller belongs to the Application Services layer. The idea behind this pattern is pretty simple, and yet quite powerful. Often we cannot use our entities and value objects as is on the user interface. It usually requires the data entities and value objects represent to be a different shape in order to be displayed to the use, so we need to transform it into something digestible for the Views. That is where our Controller come into play. They act as a mediator between the domain model and the UI. You can think of a Controller as a wrapper. It works on top of one or several entities and allows a View to easily interact with those entities. The two main elements that enable smooth communication between Views and Controller is REST. So when a user interacts with interface, for example, clicks on a button, this View then invokes controller. This technique enables loose coupling between Views and Controller .

In DDD Onion Architecture :
  * UI   = HTML
    Views

- **Application Services = Controllers**

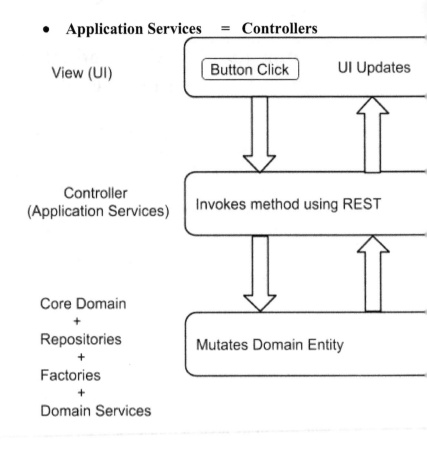

Adding UI for the Snack Machine

I've made some preparatory work. Set up a new static web project in eclipse as per the image below. This is a simple static web project containing HTML and JavaScript files only.

```
UI
  JavaScript Resources
  WebContent
    common
      jquery-3.3.1.js
    snackMachine
      snackMachine.js
      SnackMachineView.html
    utils
```

Download jquery-3.3.1.js file from
https://jquery.com/
And put it in common folder as shown above.
Here are the other files
SnackMachineView.html :

```html
<html><head></head><body>
    <table style="width:100%">
        <tbody>

            <tr>
                <td><button id="btnBuy">Buy
a Snack</button></td>


            </tr>
            <tr>
        </tr></tbody></table>
        <br>
        <br>
        <br>
        <span>Money inserted :$<span
id="moneyInserted">0</span></span>
        <br>
        <table style="width:100%">

            <tbody><tr><td><button
id="btnInsertCent">Insert 1 cent
coin</button></td>
```

```html
        <td><button id="btnInsertTenCent">Insert 10 cent coin</button></td>
        <td><button id="btnInsertQuarter">Insert 25 cent coin</button></td>
        </tr>

        <tr><td><button id="btnInsertDollar">Insert 1 dollar note</button></td>
        <td><button id="btnInsertFiveDollar">Insert 5 dollar note</button></td>
        <td><button id="btnInsertTwentyDollar">Insert 20 dollar
                note</button></td>
        </tr>
    </tbody></table>
    <br>
    <br>
    <br>
    <button id="btnReturnMoney">Return Money</button>
    <br>
    <br>
    <br>
    <br>
    <br>
    <br>
    <br>
    <br>

    <br>
```

Number of coins and Notes in SnackMachine

```html
    <table style="width:100%">
```

```html
            <tbody><tr><td>No. of 1 cent coin
: <span id="cent">0</span></td>
            <td>No. of 10 cent coin : <span
id="tenCent">0</span> </td>
            <td>No. of 25 cent coin : <span
id="quarter">0</span> </td>
            </tr>


            <tr><td>No. of 1 dollar note :
<span id="dollar">0</span></td>
            <td>No. of 5 dollar note : <span
id="fiveDollar">2</span></td>
            <td>No. of 20 dollar note : <span
id="twentyDollar">0</span></td>
            </tr>
        </tbody></table>
        <script src="../common/jquery-
3.3.1.js"></script>
        <script src="snackMachine.js"></script>
</body></html>
```

Now open this html page in a web browser like google chrome. You will see the UI like this.

Buy a Snack

Money inserted :$0

Insert 1 cent coin   Insert 10 cent coin   Insert 25 cent coin

Insert 1 dollar note   Insert 5 dollar note   Insert 20 dollar note

Return Money

Number of coins and Notes in SnackMachine

No. of 1 cent coin : 0   No. of 10 cent coin : 0   No. of 25 cent coin : 0

No. of 1 dollar note : 0   No. of 5 dollar note : 2   No. of 20 dollar note :

This is the UI itself. All the values(snack price, snack quantity, money inserted value etc) in UI are hardcoded currently. It doesn't do anything at this point, because we didn't define the required properties in the Controller yet, and that's what we're going to do here.

I added a new class .This is the Controller.

```
package ddd.logic;
import org.springframework.stereotype.Controller;
import org.springframework.web.bind.annotation.RequestMapping;
@Controller
@RequestMapping(path = "/snackmachines")
public class SnackMachineController {
}
```

We are going to build the Controller. Remember, we discussed that the Controller acts as a wrapper on top of an entity and provides the functionality required for the

View. To implement this, we need to get the entity somehow.I'm just creating a new SnackMachine object as static field here, so anytime we run the application, it will work with a new instance. We will change that when we introduce persistence for our domain model.

We will introduce a new supporting classe SnachMachineDto to controller for data transfer from server to html page.

```java
package ddd.logic;
public class SnackMachineDto {
    private Money moneyInside;
    private Money moneyInTransaction;
    private long id;

    public long getId() {
        return id;
    }
    public void setId(long id) {
        this.id = id;
    }
    public Money getMoneyInside() {
        return moneyInside;
    }
    public void setMoneyInside(Money moneyInside) {
        this.moneyInside = moneyInside;
    }
    public Money getMoneyInTransaction() {
        return moneyInTransaction;
    }
    public void setMoneyInTransaction(Money moneyInTransaction) {
        this.moneyInTransaction = moneyInTransaction;
    }
```

```java
}
public final class SnackMachine extends
Entity {
    private Money moneyInside = None;
    private Money moneyInTransaction=
None;
    public Money getMoneyInside() {
        return moneyInside;
    }
    public Money getMoneyInTransaction() {
        return moneyInTransaction;
    }
    public SnackMachineDto
convertToSnackMachineDto(){
        SnackMachineDto
snackMachineDto = new SnackMachineDto();
snackMachineDto.setId(snackMachine.getId()
);
snackMachineDto.setMoneyInside(snackMach
ine.getMoneyInside());
        snackMachineDto.setMoneyInTrans
action(snackMachine.getMoneyInTransaction
());
        return snackMachineDto;
    }
    // all other codes are same as above
SnackMachine class
}
package ddd.logic;
import
org.springframework.stereotype.Controller;
import
org.springframework.web.bind.annotation.Ge
tMapping;
import
org.springframework.web.bind.annotation.Re
questMapping;
```

```java
import
org.springframework.web.bind.annotation.Re
sponseBody;
@Controller
@RequestMapping(path = "/snackmachines")
public class SnackMachineController {
    static SnackMachine snackMachine =
new SnackMachine();   // We will change this
when we
 //introduce persistence for our domain model.
    @GetMapping("/{id}")
    @ResponseBody
    public SnackMachineDto
getSnackMachine(@PathVariable("id") long
id) {
    return
snackMachine.convertToSnackMachineDto();
    }
}
```

All right, so let's start off by displaying the amount of money we inserted into the machine. It will be shown here near the money inserted label. This label is bound to the moneyInTransaction property, so we need to do the following changes.

snackMachine.js :

```javascript
const rootURI =
"http://localhost:8080/snackmachines/1";
getSnachMachine();
function getSnachMachine(){
    $.get(rootURI, function(data,
status){        $('#moneyInserted').html(dat
a.moneyInTransaction.amount);
$('#cent').html(data.oneCentCount);
        $('#tenCent').html(data.tenCentCou
nt);
        $('#quarter').html(data.quarterCoun
t);
```

```
        $('#dollar').html(data.oneDollarCou
nt);
        $('#fiveDollar').html(data.fiveDollar
Count);
        $('#twentyDollar').html(data.twenty
DollarCount);
    });
}
```

Now we will the application by running the LogicApplication.java

Class as run as java application.

Note : Using Window command prompt, you can also build the project using command "gradlew clean build" at location "C:\logic" and run using"java -jar logic-0.0.1-SNAPSHOT" at location "C:\logic\build\libs";

Now if we run the application, and open the SnackMachineView.html page in browser ,you can see the money inserted is displayed and is currently 0. The problem is that it doesn't change if we try to put money in, so let's fix that.

The button that puts the coins and note into the machine is bound to inserMoney() method of controller, which in turn will insert to the snack machine.

We change the files as below :

snachMachine.js :

```
$("button").click(function() {
    switch (this.id) {
    case "btnInsertCent" :
        insert("Cent")
      break;
    case "btnInsertTenCent" :
        insert("TenCent")
      break;
    case "btnInsertQuarter" :
        insert("Quarter")
      break;
```

```
        case "btnInsertDollar" :
            insert("Dollar")
          break;
        case "btnInsertFiveDollar" :
            insert("FiveDollar")
          break;
        case "btnInsertTwentyDollar" :
            insert("TwentyDollar")
          break
        default :
          break;
    }
});
function insert(coinOrNote){
    $.ajax({
      url:
rootURI+'/moneyInTransaction/'+coinOrNote
,
      type: 'PUT',
      success: function(result) {
          // Do something with the result
      }
    });
    location.reload();
}
//rest of the code of snackmachine.js are same
as above
public class SnackMachineController
{       @PutMapping("/{id}/moneyInTransacti
on/{coinOrNote}")
      public void
inserMoney(@PathVariable("id") long id,
@PathVariable("coinOrNote") String
coinOrNote) {
          if(coinOrNote.equalsIgnoreCase("Ce
nt")) snackMachine.insertMoney(Cent);
          else
if(coinOrNote.equalsIgnoreCase("TenCent"))
snackMachine.insertMoney(TenCent);
```

```
        else
if(coinOrNote.equalsIgnoreCase("Quarter"))
snackMachine.insertMoney(Quarter);
        else
if(coinOrNote.equalsIgnoreCase("Dollar"))
snackMachine.insertMoney(Dollar);
        else
if(coinOrNote.equalsIgnoreCase("FiveDollar"
)) snackMachine.insertMoney(FiveDollar);
        else
if(coinOrNote.equalsIgnoreCase("TwentyDoll
ar"))
snackMachine.insertMoney(TwentyDollar);
    }
}
```

We also need to notify the View so that it refreshes the whole page. So now if we try to put money into the machine, you can see the money actually goes there. The money inserted label displays that.

The next thing to consider is the Return money button. Let's add a method in controller for it. The method itself calls the appropriate method on the SnackMachine class. If I put 11 cents into the machine and return them back, you can see the money inserted turns back to 0.

```
public class SnackMachineController {
    @PutMapping("/{id}/moneyInTransactio
n")
    public void
returnMoney(@PathVariable("id") long id) {
        snackMachine.returnMoney();
    }
// rest of the codes are same
}
```

snackMachinejs :

```
$("button").click(function() {
    switch (this.id) {
```

```
    case "btnReturnMoney" :
        returnMoney()
      break;
      default :
      break;
  }
});
function returnMoney(){
  $.ajax({
    url: rootURI+'/moneyInTransaction',
    type: 'PUT',
    success: function(result) {
      // Do something with the result
    }
  });
  location.reload();
}
```

//all other codes are same as above js file
Very well, the last thing we need to do here is we need to implement the buying functionality. In it, we need to delegate the execution to the SnackMachine entity, tell the user they have both a snack, and once again notify the View about both of the properties. Now if I insert, for example, three dollars, and buy a snack, you can see the money inserted is discarded, which means all inserted money are now the property of the machine, and we cannot retrieve them back. In contrast, if I insert some money and return it, both the money inserted and the money inside revert to the initial values.

snackMachine.js :

```
$("button").click(function() {
  switch (this.id) {
  case "btnBuyChocolate" :
      buy("1")
    break;
    default :
```

```
      break;
   }
});
function buy(position){
   $.ajax({
      url: rootURI+'/'+position,
      type: 'PUT',
      success: function(result) {}
   });
   location.reload();
}
// all other codes are same as in above js file
public class SnackMachineController {
      // all other codes are same as in above
controller
      @PutMapping("/{id}/{slotNumber}")
      public void
buySnack(@PathVariable("id") long id,
@PathVariable("slotNumber") int
slotNumber) {
            snackMachine.buySnack();
   }
// we will use slotNumber in future
//rest codes are same as in above
SnackMachineController .java
}
```

In the insertMoney method, the name of the input parameter doesn't actually reflect the meaning of it. We are not inserting just some arbitrary money inside the machine. We can only insert a single coin or a single note. So let's rename it to insertCoinOrNote.

Recap: Adding UI for the Snack Machine

We saw we built a UI and Application Services layer. In our case, the UI layer was represented by HTML Views, Application Services layer by Spring boot spring REST Controller. The Application Services layer usually acts as a mediator between the outside world, which is user interface, and the domain layer. This layer itself shouldn't contain any business logic, only coordinate the communication between different elements of the domain and validate the inputs from the UI. In our case, the Controller we created acts as a wrapper on top of an entity. It augments it with the functionality required for the view. It didn't contain any business logic, but rather delegated it to the entity. Application Services can work with other domain classes as well, such as repositories. We will see it later in this module. It's important to find a proper place for the logic we are adding to our code base. Some of it makes sense in the domain layer. For example, if you want to show dollar or cent sign on view we can implement the ToString method as part of the Money class.

- As part of the domain layer:

```
@Override
    public String toString(){
        if (getAmount() < 1)
            return "¢" + getAmount()* 100;
        return "$" + getAmount();
    }
```

Other logic looks better as part of the Application Services layer. For instance, if we want to show all money (money inside + money in transaction) on view, we can add it as a part of the Controller.

- As part of the application layer:

```
public Money getWholeMoney() {
        return Money.add(moneyInside,
moneyInTransaction);
    }
```

You can use the following rule of thumb when you want to decide between the two. If the piece of logic you are looking at makes sense only in the context of UI, then it's probably better to place it into an Application Service, Controller in our case, otherwise, it should be part of the domain layer.

- Try to put logic to a proper layer of abstraction

Designing the Database for the Snack Machine

It's a good time now to discuss the database design for our domain model. We currently have only two classes in it, SnackMachine and Money.

```
public final class SnackMachine extends
Entity{
    public Money moneyInside;
    public Money moneyInTransaction;
}
public classMoney extends ValueObject{
    public int oneCentCount;
    public int tenCentCount;
    public int quarterCount;
    public int oneDollarCount;
    public int fiveDollarCount;
```

```
    public int twentyDollarCount;
}
```
We need to decide which of their properties we want to persist in the database. That is another subject for discussion with a domain expert, because such decisions would affect the overall model behavior. For example, if we decide to store both money properties, that would mean we want to save the model's state not only between the transactions, but also in the middle of it. Let's assume that we, together with a domain expert, decided to be persist moneyInTransaction and moneyInside.

```
public classSnackMachine extends Entity{
    public Money moneyInside;
    public Money moneyInTransaction ;
}
public classMoney extends ValueObject{
    public int oneCentCount;
    public int tenCentCount;
    public int quarterCount;
    public int oneDollarCount;
    public int fiveDollarCount;
    public int twentyDollarCount;
}
```
How would the database look in this case? One of the options that might come to mind is to create separate tables for each of them, like this.

SnackMachine

PK	snackMachineID
	moneyID

Money

PK	moneyID

93

oneCentCount
tenCentCount
quarterCount
oneDollarCount
fiveDollarCount

You can see the SnackMachine table in this diagram contains a reference to the Money table. While these might seem a good idea, such a design has two major drawbacks. First of all, the Money table contains an identifier. It means that we will have to introduce a separate ID field in our domain model in order to be able to work with such a table correctly. This in turn means that we need to give the Money ValueObject some identity, and that violates the definition of value object. The other drawback is that with this solution, we can potentially detach value objects from entities. The Money ValueObject can live by its own, because we are able to delete a SnackMachine role from the database without deleting a corresponding Money role. That would be a violation of another rule, which states that the lifetime of value object should fully depend on the lifetime of the apparent entities. It turns out that the best solution in this case is to inline the fields from the Money table to the SnackMachine table, like this. This would solve all the problems I stated earlier. We don't give an identity to the Money ValueObject, and its lifetime now fully depends on the lifetime of the SnackMachine Entity. And it makes sense if you mentally replace all the fields that regard to Money with a single integer, as I suggested in the previous module. Do you create a separate table for an integer? Of course not. You just inline that integer to the table you want it to be in. The same applies to the ValueObjects. Don't introduce separate tables for them, just inline them into the parent entities table.

SnackMachine

PK	snackMachineID
	oneCentCount
	tenCentCount
	quarterCount
	oneDollarCount
	fiveDollarCount
	twentyDollarCount

By the way we do not need to explicitly create the tables in database . Spring boot will do it for us . We will see in next chapter.

So now as we've come up with a database structure for our domain model, let's see how to link them together.

Introducing an ORM

In this book, we'll be using Spring boot JPA as an object-relational mapper, we have added JPA and database H2 as project dependencies at the beginning of the project generation from the Spring initialiser website. We will talk about different mapping structures in a few minutes.

ID Generation Strategies

There are three popular methods to
implement ID generation for domain entities
with SQL database. One of them is to rely on
the SQL database's id generation feature.

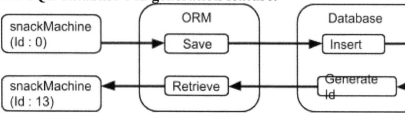

We can define an ID column in such a way
that every time we insert a new snackmachine,
SQL database will attach a new identifier to it.
So when we create a new entity in the memory
and then save it, the ORM pushes a new insert
to the database. The database generates a new
identifier, which the ORM then retrieves and
assigns to the entity in the memory. While this
solution allows us to leverage the built-in SQL
database functionality and generate good-
looking integer values, it has a major
drawback. In order to actually sign an
identifier to an entity, Hibernate has to
perform a roundtrip to the database and that
doesn't play well with the concept of unit of
work. It means that in some cases, we are no
longer able to execute all changes made during
a session at once.
Another way to generate an identifier is to use
UUIDs on client side.
UUIDs:
public abstract class Entity{
        private UUID id;
        private Entity() {

96

```
                    id= UUID.randomUUID();
        }
        public UUID getId(){
                return id;
        }
}
```

1BA876A6-2D12-3CB3-CFF3-7A82A57B0863
It doesn't contain the drawback I described, because UUIDs can be easily generated on the client side, so there is no need to make a roundtrip to the server. The only shortcoming with this approach is UUIDs themselves. They may be cumbersome to work with, and you might prefer to have integer identifiers instead. If this is the case, you can use the third option, Hi/Lo algorithm.

Hilo generator :

hilo is a shortcut name for TableHiloGenerator class. It is some thing different, when compared to other generator classes. Let us see how it is differ with others. Generally speaking, it is mostly a matter of taste whether you choose UUIDs or Hi/Lo. For this book, I use the @GeneratedValue by JPA, but it's perfectly fine if you prefer UUIDs instead.

Mapping Strategies

- **XML files**
- **Annotations**

There are two approaches when it comes to mapping domain entities to tables in the database, XML files, and annotations mapping. XML files are quite verbose and are prone to break when refactoring, because they operate literal strings to define the names of the properties being mapped. Annotation is a better option. They don't have the shortcomings of XML files, but they do have another one. Remember, we talked about the importance of isolation. We discussed that the innermost layer of the onion architecture, entities, value objects, aggregates, and domain events, should have a single responsibility, which is representing the domain knowledge of your system. Add in mapping attributes directly to entities, means they start holding the knowledge about how they are being stored in the database. Therefore, this mapping strategy violates this single responsibility principle. So will use annotations but not on Core domain classes like SnackMachine.java. We will use DTOes like SnackMachineDto

```
package ddd.logic;
import javax.persistence.Entity;
import javax.persistence.GeneratedValue;
import javax.persistence.Id;
@Entity
public class SnackMachineDto {
    @Id
    @GeneratedValue
    private long id;
    private int oneCentCount;
    private int tenCentCount;
    private int quarterCount;
    private int oneDollarCount;
    private int fiveDollarCount;
    private int twentyDollarCount;
    private float moneyInTransaction;
    // generate public getters & setters for all the fields
}
```

Modify application.properties as shown below:
spring.h2.console.enabled=true
logging.level.org.hibernate.SQL=debug
logging.level.org.hibernate.type.descriptor.sql
=trace
Now the run the LogicApplication.java as java application
When you start the application up now, you would see a lot of magic unfold!
When you reload the application, you can launch up H2 Console at
http://localhost:8080/h2-console.

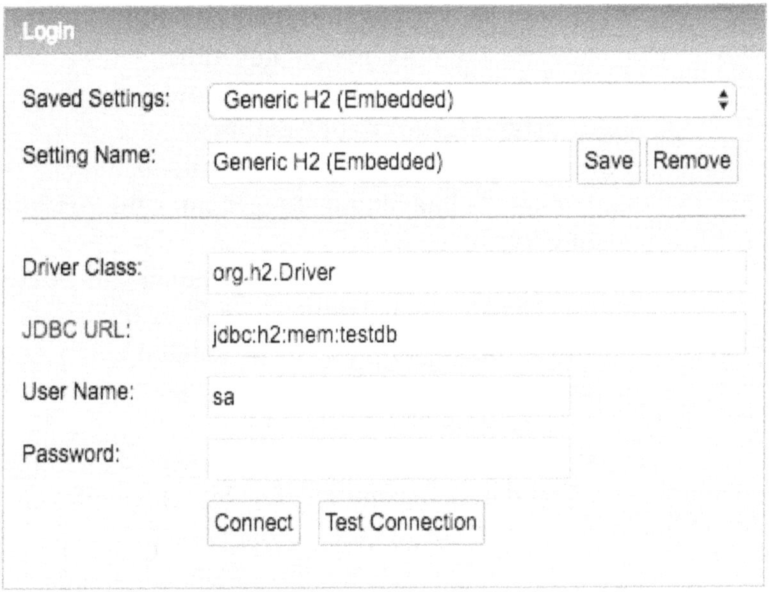

Make sure that you use
jdbc:h2:mem:testdb as JDBC URL.
Click on the connect button.
You will see that a new table called SnackMachineDto is created in H2 Console automatically by Spring Boot JPA.
Now execute the below SQL query in this H2 console :

insert into snack_machine_dto
(five_dollar_count, money_in_transaction,
one_cent_count, one_dollar_count,
quarter_count, ten_cent_count,
twenty_dollar_count, id) values (1, 0.0, 1, 1, 1,
1, 1, 1);
So now every time you restart this Spring boot
application
These two queries will automatically executed
:
drop table snack_machine_dto if exists
create table snack_machine_dto (id bigint not
null, five_dollar_count integer not null,
money_in_transaction float not null,
one_cent_count integer not null,
one_dollar_count integer not null,
quarter_count integer not null,
ten_cent_count integer not null,
twenty_dollar_count integer not null, primary
key (id))
You can see every time you restart this Spring
boot application all the records of the table
snack_machine_dto will be deleted .
So every time we start the application we need
to execute :
insert into snack_machine_dto
(five_dollar_count, money_in_transaction,
one_cent_count, one_dollar_count,
quarter_count, ten_cent_count,
twenty_dollar_count, id) values (1, 0.0, 1, 1, 1,
1, 1, 1);
In the H2 console

Putting It All Together

Now as we've set up persistence for our domain model, let's incorporate it into our UI layer. Currently Controller creates a SnackMachine in static block. We can replace it with a SnackMachine taken from the database, fetching the machine from the DB, and passing it to the View.

```
package ddd.logic;
import
org.springframework.data.repository.CrudRepository;
public interface SnackMachineRepository
extends CrudRepository<SnackMachineDto,
Long> {
}
public class SnackMachineController {
    @Autowired
    SnackMachineRepository
snackMachineRepository;
    @GetMapping("/{id}")
    @ResponseBody
    public SnackMachineDto
getSnackMachine(@PathVariable("id") long
id) {
    return
snackMachineRepository.findById(id).orElse(
null);
    }
    @PutMapping("/{id}/{slotNumber}")
    public void
buySnack(@PathVariable("id") long id,
@PathVariable("slotNumber") int
slotNumber) {
```

```java
        SnackMachineDto snackMachineDto
=
snackMachineRepository.findById(id).orElse(
null);
        SnackMachine snackMachine =
snackMachineDto.convertToSnackMachine();

        snackMachine.buySnack();
        snackMachineRepository.save(snack
Machine.convertToSnackMachineDto());
    }

    @PutMapping("/{id}/moneyInTransactio
n/{coinOrNote}")
    public void
insertCoinOrNote(@PathVariable("id") long
id, @PathVariable("coinOrNote") String
coinOrNote) {
        SnackMachineDto snackMachineDto
=
snackMachineRepository.findById(id).orElse(
null);
        SnackMachine snackMachine =
snackMachineDto.convertToSnackMachine();

        if(coinOrNote.equalsIgnoreCase("Ce
nt")) snackMachine.insertMoney(Cent);
        else
if(coinOrNote.equalsIgnoreCase("TenCent"))
snackMachine.insertMoney(TenCent);
        else
if(coinOrNote.equalsIgnoreCase("Quarter"))
snackMachine.insertMoney(Quarter);
        else
if(coinOrNote.equalsIgnoreCase("Dollar"))
snackMachine.insertMoney(Dollar);
        else
if(coinOrNote.equalsIgnoreCase("FiveDollar"
)) snackMachine.insertMoney(FiveDollar);
```

```java
        else
if(coinOrNote.equalsIgnoreCase("TwentyDoll
ar"))
snackMachine.insertMoney(TwentyDollar);

        snackMachineRepository.save(snack
Machine.convertToSnackMachineDto());
    }
    @PutMapping("/{id}/moneyInTransactio
n")
    public void
returnMoney(@PathVariable("id") long id) {
        SnackMachineDto snackMachineDto
=
snackMachineRepository.findById(id).orElse(
null);
        SnackMachine snackMachine =
snackMachineDto.convertToSnackMachine();

        snackMachine.returnMoney();
        snackMachineRepository.save(snack
Machine.convertToSnackMachineDto());
    }
}
public class SnackMachine {
    public SnackMachineDto
convertToSnackMachineDto() {
        SnackMachineDto snackMachineDto
= new SnackMachineDto();
        snackMachineDto.setId(id);
        snackMachineDto.setMoneyInTrans
action(moneyInTransaction);        snackMachi
neDto.setOneCentCount(moneyInside.getOne
CentCount());        snackMachineDto.setTenC
entCount(moneyInside.getTenCentCount());
    snackMachineDto.setQuarterCount(money
Inside.getQuarterCount());        snackMa
chineDto.setOneDollarCount(moneyInside.get
OneDollarCount());        snackMachineDto.set
```

```
            FiveDollarCount(moneyInside.getFiveDollarC
ount());
            snackMachineDto.setTwentyDollarC
ount(moneyInside.getTwentyDollarCount());
            return snackMachineDto;
    }
//rest are same
}
public class SnackMachineDto {
    public SnackMachine
convertToSnackMachine() {
            SnackMachine snackMachine = new
SnackMachine();
            snackMachine.setId(id);        snackM
achine.setMoneyInTransaction(moneyInTrans
action);
            snackMachine.setMoneyInside(new
Money(oneCentCount,tenCentCount,quarter
Count,           oneDollarCount,fiveDolla
rCount,twentyDollarCount));
            return snackMachine;
    }
// rest are same
}
```

If I run the application, you can see the SnackMachine contains one piece of each coin and note. It means they are successfully taken from the database. We can see we are saving the SnackMachine after purchase is completed.

Let's see if it works. If I insert, for example, 3 cents and click on the Buy button, the new amount of money should be persisted in the database, and it is. You can see there are four 1 cent coins now attached to the SnackMachine. Perfect. Our first draft of the SnackMachine is ready, and we can move on and build up new functionality on top of it.

Summary

- View and controller pattern in Onion Architecture
- Try to put logic to a proper layer of abstraction
- Value Objects shouldn't have their own tables
- Purity trade-offs when using an ORM
- Id generation strategies
- Mapping strategies

In this module, we introduced UI and persistence layers for our application. We discussed the View and controller design pattern and where they belong in the onion architecture. We talked about the importance of finding a proper place for the logic we are adding to our code base. We've discussed the database for the snack machine. We talked about best practices for persistence value objects. They shouldn't have their own tables, but rather be inlined in the parent entities table. You saw how to use an ORM to persist the domain model, and also what changes must be made in order to comply with the Hibernate requirements. For example, we had to make the SnackMachine entity un final , and required getters and setters . I believe it is still a good tradeoff. ORMs free us from a lot of manual work on one hand and allow us to maintain a good degree of isolation for our domain model on the other. We discussed pros and cons of different Id generation strategies. We also looked at mapping strategies and saw what is the best feed for us and why. Finally, we put all pieces together and saw how our domain model is displayed and being persisted in practice. In the next module, we will talk about other two fundamental DDD concepts, aggregates and repositories, and we'll see how to apply them to our project.

Module 4: Extending the Bounded Context with Aggregates

Introduction

In this module, we will extend our SnackMachine model with the actual purchase functionality. Along the way, we will discuss best practices for working with aggregates, and we'll see how they are applicable to our project.

- Purchase functionality
- Aggregates

Problem Description

- 3 slots of snacks

- Return the change
- Check if inserted money is enough and the slot isn't empty
- Check if there's enough change

Currently our SnackMachine model doesn't actually make any purchases, it just appropriates whatever money a user inserted without giving anything back. Obviously that's not how real snack machines work, and we need to extend the model's functionality. So, what are the requirements for the functionality we need to implement? First of all, the snack machine should have three slots, each of which may contain several snacks of the same type and of the same price. The snack machine should allow us to buy any item from those slots. There are several business rules that should be followed here. First of all, if a user inserts more money than needed, the machine must return back the change. If the money inserted is not enough, or there are no products left in the slot, the user should get an error message. And finally, it might happen that there is not enough change in the machine. We should handle such situations as well. As usual, we will start with the simplest implementation possible and iteratively move towards a better design. We will see how to handle one 1-to-many relationships between domain classes, how to combine several entities into aggregates, and how to find proper boundaries for them.

Scope for the Module :

- Iterative approach to design
- 1-to-many relationships
- Combining several entities into aggregates

Starting with the Implementation

Let's see how we can implement the new requirements in code. This is how our domain model looks like currently.

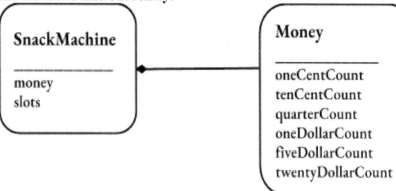

To handle the new purchase functionality, we need to add two new entities, snack and slot.

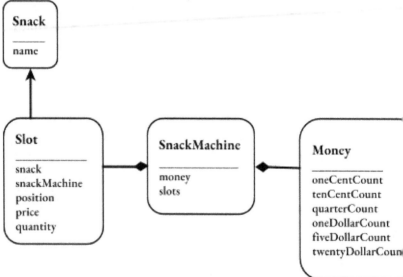

The Snack class will contain only Name field. The Slot entity should have links to both a

Snack and a SnackMachine, and also contain the information about the slot, its position in the machine, and the price and the number of the snacks residing in the slot. All right, let's add a new class, Snack.

```
package ddd.logic;
public class Snack extends Entity {
    private String name;
    public String getName() {
        return name;
    }
    public void setName(String name) {
        this.name = name;
    }
    private Snack() {
    }
    private Snack(String name) {
        this.name = name;
    }
}
```

This would be an entity, so I'm inheriting it from the Entity base class. And it will contain only a single name property. Another entity we need to introduce is Slot.

```
package ddd.logic;
public class Slot extends Entity {
    private Snack snack;
    private int quantity;
    private float price;
    private SnackMachine snackMachine;
    private int position;
    public Slot() {
    }
    public Slot(SnackMachine snackMachine,
int position, Snack snack, int quantity, float
price) {
        this.snackMachine = snackMachine;
        this.position = position;
        this.snack = snack;
```

```java
            this.quantity = quantity;
            this.price = price;
        }
        public Snack getSnack() {
            return snack;
        }
        public void setSnack(Snack snack) {
            this.snack = snack;
        }
        public int getQuantity() {
            return quantity;
        }
        public void setQuantity(int quantity) {
            this.quantity = quantity;
        }
        public float getPrice() {
            return price;
        }
        public void setPrice(float price) {
            this.price = price;
        }
        public SnackMachine getSnackMachine()
{
            return snackMachine;
        }
        public void
setSnackMachine(SnackMachine
snackMachine) {
            this.snackMachine = snackMachine;
        }
        public int getPosition() {
            return position;
        }
        public void setPosition(int position) {
            this.position = position;
        }
}
```

Here are its properties. And I have to add two constructors here as well, a default one, and the one which accepts all properties required to initialize a slot. This is the SnackMachine class. We'll start by modifying the existing test that covers the buySnack method. Let's rename it from money_in_transaction_goes_to_money_inside _after_purchase to buySnack_trades_inserted_money_for_a_snack.

```
@Test
    public void
buySnack_trades_inserted_money_for_a_snack() {
        SnackMachine snackMachine = new SnackMachine();
        snackMachine.loadSnacks(1, new Snack("Some snack"), 10, 1));
        snackMachine.insertMoney(Dollar);
        snackMachine.buySnack(1);
assertEquals(snackMachine.getMoneyInTransaction(),
0);      assertEquals(snackMachine.getMoneyInside().getAmount(), 1, 0.5);
        Slot slot = snackMachine.getSlots().stream().filter(x -> x.getPosition() == 1).findAny().orElse(null);
assertEquals(slot.getQuantity(), 1);
    }
```

First of all, before we buy anything, we need to put snacks into it somehow, so we'll need to implement a corresponding method. And two, we'll need to validate that the number of snacks decreased after the purchase.

All right, creating the loadSnacks method, the Slot number where we need to put the snacks, a snack instance, quantity, and price. In order to implement this method, we need to introduce a storage for the snacks, so I'm adding a corresponding property, which

111

would hold the slots the machine has. It is of type List. Now we can find a slot base position and assign a new snack, quantity, and price to it.

```java
public class SnackMachine extends Entity {
    private Money moneyInside = None;
    private Money moneyInTransaction= None;
    private List<Slot> slots;

    public List<Slot> getSlots() {
        return slots;
    }
    public void setSlots(List<Slot> slots) {
        this.slots = slots;
    }
    public void loadSnacks(int position, Snack snack, int quantity, float price) {
        Slot slot = slots.stream().filter(x -> x.getPosition() == position).findAny().orElse(null);
        if(slot != null) {
            slot.setSnack(snack);
            slot.setQuantity(quantity);
            slot.setPrice(price);
        }
    }
// remain codes are same as previous
}
```

All right, we can load some snacks to the first slot of the machine with quantity 10 and price 1 dollar. We'll need only a single dollar to buy this snack. Note that we currently call the buySnack method without any parameters. We need to somehow specify what snack we are buying. The best way to do this is to pass the position of the slot, because that's exactly how the end user would approach the task. He or she just needs to indicate in what slot they are interested in is located. We've loaded the snack into the first slot, so I'm passing one here as well. And now we can verify that the number of the snacks has changed. It should be nine after the purchase. All right, let's make our code compile by adding a position parameter to this method. I need to define a constructor and assign a new list to the property. Every snack machine in our domain model will have exactly three slots, so we can initialize all of them manually here, passing these as a SnackMachine instance to the slot, the position is 1, no snacks, and 0 for both the quantity and the price. The other two slots are the same, except that they are located at different positions. And just to be consistent with the way we initialize the SnackMachine instances, I'll move these two lines to the constructor as well. The quantity of the snacks in the slot didn't decrease as we expected. To fix this, we need to go to the BuySnack method and reduce the snack number by one.

```java
public class SnackMachine extends Entity {
    private Money moneyInside;
    private Money moneyInTransaction;
    private List<Slot> slots;

    public SnackMachine() {
        moneyInside = None;
        moneyInTransaction = None;
        slots = new ArrayList<>();
        slots.add(new Slot(this, 1, null, 0, 1));
        slots.add(new Slot(this, 2, null, 0, 1));
        slots.add(new Slot(this, 3, null, 0, 1));
    }

    public void buySnack(int position) {
```

```
        Slot slot = slots.stream().filter(x ->
x.getPosition() ==
position).findAny().orElse(null);
            slot.setQuantity(slot.getQuantity()-
1);
        moneyInside =
Money.add(moneyInside,
moneyInTransaction);
        moneyInTransaction = None;
    }
//remaining codes are same
}
```

As you can tell, the buySnack method still
lacks some functionality. For example, we
didn't return change and we don't have any
validations in place. We will address this issue
soon. For now, let's take a minute and discuss
the design we've come up with.

Aggregates

- **Snack machine and Snack are two
  aggregates**

At this point, we approached an important
topic, the notion of aggregate. In our domain
model, there are two of them, snack machine
and snack. Let's elaborate on that.

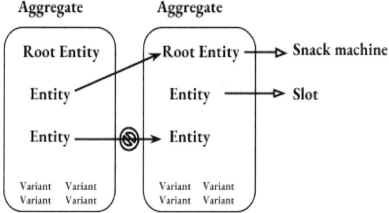

Aggregate is a design pattern that helps us simplify the domain model by gathering multiple entities under a single abstraction. This concept includes several implications. First of all, an aggregate is a conceptual whole, meaning that it represents a cohesive notion of the domain model. Every aggregate has a set of invariants, which it maintains during its lifetime. It means that in any given time, an aggregate should reside in a valid state. For example, let's say snacks have an additional attribute, weight, and we have an invariant stating that our snack machine cannot hold more than 10 pounds of snacks. This kind of validation should be performed in the aggregate so that it's not possible for the client code to add more snacks if the overall weight exceeds the limit. Every aggregate should have a root. That is, the entity which is the domain for the aggregate, so to speak. An important rule regarding this notion is that classes outside of the aggregate can only reference the root of that aggregate. They cannot hold a permanent reference to other entities of the aggregate. In our case, the root of the snack machine aggregate is the SnackMachine class. It means that entities outside this aggregate cannot keep a link to the slot entity. They can hold it temporarily, though. For example, in a local variable during some method, but they should get access to it via the root entity only. So, in our case, if a client code is about to get information about some slot from the database, it should get the corresponding snack machine instance first, and only after that retrieve the required slot using the root entity. However, try to avoid exposing the internal entities at all if possible. You will see this practice in a minute. We will hide the slot entity from the outside world completely. This point strongly correlates with the previous one. Restricting access to the entities that are internal to an aggregate helps protect the aggregate's invariants. Ideally there should be no way for the client code to break the aggregate's invariants and thus corrupt its internal state.

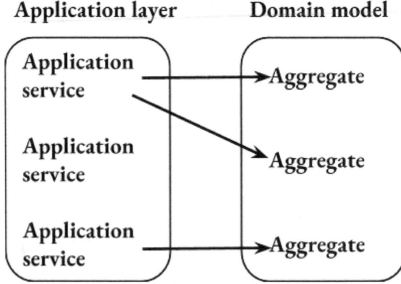

Aggregates also act as a single operational unit for the code in your application layer.

Application Services should retrieve them from the database, perform actions, and store them back as a single object. In other words, they should consider an aggregate a conceptual whole and refrain from working with separate entities in it. Another function aggregates hold is maintaining consistency boundaries. It means that in any given time the data in the database that belong to a single aggregate should be consistent. To achieve this, we need to persist an aggregate in a transactional manner.

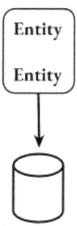

In our case, there shouldn't be a situation where we save to the database only the snack machine itself without saving its slots with it. The database should contain all information about the aggregate and this information must be consistent, meaning that it shouldn't break the invariants of this aggregate. At the same time, the invariants that span across several aggregates shouldn't be expected to be up-to-date all the time. They can be eventually consistent.

- Entity can belong to a single aggregate only

- Value object can belong to multiple aggregates

Note that while an entity can belong to only a single aggregate, a value object can reside in several aggregates. For example, there might be another aggregate and an entity in it that holds a money property. That's perfectly fine. Again, it makes sense if you replace the money value object with an integer, and an entity in your domain model can hold one. The same rules are applicable to value objects.

How to Find Boundaries for Aggregates

One of the biggest questions that arrives when it comes to working with aggregates is how to choose boundaries for them. Why are there exactly two aggregates in our domain model and not, say, one or three? We could, for example, make all three entities belong to a single aggregate, so why is it that we have such boundaries in our domain model? Just like with entities and value objects, there are no objective traits that make particular boundaries for an aggregate. They fully depend on the domain model you are working in. The way we group entities into aggregates in different domain models can vary a lot, even if those models have the same set of entities.

- Entities inside comprise a cohesive group of classes
- Entities in different aggregates should maintain loose coupling among each other

However, there are some guidelines you can follow in order to identify the boundaries. Domain attributes that makes an aggregate is cohesion of the entities in it. Entities inside the same aggregate should be highly cohesive, whereas entities in different aggregates should maintain loose coupling among each other. It's a good practice to ask yourself the following question, does an entity make sense without some other entity? If it does, then it should probably be the root of its own aggregate. Otherwise, it should be a part of some other existing aggregate.

- Snack machine + Slot = Aggregate 1
- Snack = Aggregate 2

In our case, the slot entity cannot exist without a snack machine, so it has to be a part of its aggregate. These two entities, SnackMachine and Slot, comprise a cohesive group of classes, an aggregate. At the same time, the Snack class can probably live by its own, so it should be the root of an aggregate, which consists of a single entity. As you go along with the development process, you will receive more information about the domain.

- Don't hesitate to change boundaries when you discover more information

If you think the boundaries you selected initially don't play well with the problem you are solving, don't hesitate to change them. Domain modeling is an iterative process, so don't expect to find proper boundaries for all your aggregates right away.

- Don't create aggregates that are too large

Be aware of creating aggregates that are too large. It might be tempting to include into aggregates more entities. For example, one could decide to include the Snack class into the SnackMachine aggregate. While it might seem a good idea, because it leaves us with less number of aggregates and thus with a simple domain model, in most cases, it doesn't work out well. The reason here is that the bigger your aggregates are, the harder it is to maintain their consistency and handle conflicts when several transactions try to update parts of a single aggregate at once. Finding proper boundaries is a tricky question, and basically is a tradeoff between the simplicity of the model and its performance characteristics.

- Most aggregates consist of 1 or 2 entities
- 3 entities per aggregate is usually a max
- The number of Value Objects per aggregate is unlimited

Most of the aggregates contains one or two entities, and I don't remember an aggregate with more than three entities in it. It's totally fine to have a lot of single entity aggregates, so don't try to gather entities into aggregates artificially. Just follow the guideline and make sure entities in your aggregates comprise a conceptual whole, meaning that they don't make a lot of sense without each other. Note that this heuristic doesn't include value objects. You can have as many value objects in your aggregates as you want.

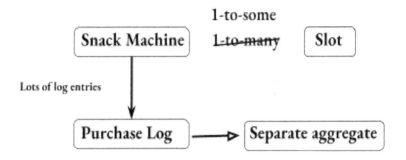

I'd like to make an important note here about 1-to-many relationships between entities. In our domain model, the relation between the SnackMachine and the Slot classes is 1-to-many, in a sense that a single machine can theoretically hold as many slots as possible. Despite its name, in most cases, the 1-to-many relation should be viewed as 1-to-some, meaning that there shouldn't be a lot of entities on the many side. If you find a class in your domain model holding a collection of entities and that collection contains more than, say, 30 members, it's a strong sign you should revisit the model and probably remove the collection and extract the entity on the many side to its own aggregate. For example, we could hold a lot of all purchases made in a snack machine as a collection in the machine itself. This design might seem compelling at first, but the problem here is that the bigger the log gets, the harder it is to maintain proper performance when working with the aggregate. In this case, it would be a good idea

121

to extract this class in a separate aggregate and work with it apart from the snack machine. To make this separation work, we could employ domain events. We will talk about domain events in the future modules.

Aggregate Root Base Class

```
public abstract class AggregateRoot extends
Entity {
    private  int version ;
    private List<DomainEvent>  events = new
ArrayList<>();
    //public getters & setters for version &
events
}
public class SnackMachine extends
AggregateRoot {}
```

As we've discussed earlier, every aggregate should have a root entity, the entity which is the main for this aggregate, and which can be referenced by entities and value objects in other aggregates. It's a good idea to create an aggregate root base class, just as we did with entities and value objects. The aggregate root base class usually has three goals. The first one is to explicitly show the boundaries of the aggregates in your domain model. By inheriting an entity from the AggregateRoot base class, you make it easier to read your code base and see which entities are roots of their own aggregates and which are just part of existing ones. Secondly, if you employ optimistic locking, you need to somehow version the entire aggregate. The best way to implement such versioning is to put a version

property to the AggregateRoot, like this. And
finally, the AggregateRoot base class is a
perfect place to hold domain events that
happen to an aggregate during its lifetime. We
will dive into this topic in much more detail in
the future modules. For now, I leave the base
class empty. We will extend it later on. Note
that if you don't need to implement optimistic
locking, and you don't use domain events in
your code base, it might be just fine to omit
the use of this base class, as it doesn't provide
much value in such situations. If this is the
case for your project, try to weigh the pros
and cons and decide whether you want to
introduce the additional base class to a
domain model or you can get away without it.
In our project, we will need it for holding
domain events, but it might be another case in
your situation.

Refactoring the Snack Machine Aggregate

Let's look at our code base in light of what we
know about aggregates. First of all, we know
that the SnackMachine and Snack entities are
the roots of their own aggregates, so let's mark
them appropriately. I changed the class they
inherit from to AggregateRoot.

```
public abstract class AggregateRoot extends
Entity {}
public class Snack extends AggregateRoot {
    // rest is same as above
}
public class SnackMachine extends
AggregateRoot {
```

```
// rest is same as above
}
```

There are two other flows in our code, namely in this particular property. Do you see them? Try to think a minute. All right, so the first drawback here is that we expose the collection (List<Slot> slots) to the outside world. The client code can easily add new elements to the collection and thus corrupt the internal state of the aggregate, namely the addition of a new slot here would violate the invariant stating that the SnackMachine can have only three slots in it. The second shortcoming is more subtle. The problem here is that we expose the Slot entity itself. As I mentioned earlier, it is a good idea to keep the entities that are not aggregates roots inside the boundaries of their aggregates, and not show them to other aggregates. It's not always possible to avoid such exposure of book, but it is in our case, as you will see. A solution here is to just make the collection private and remove getter & setters and hide it from the client code completely. You can see our test doesn't compile anymore, because it cannot access the slot collection (snackMachine.getSlots()) as we remove getter getSlots().

```java
package ddd.test;
import static org.junit.Assert.assertEquals;
import static ddd.logic.Money.Dollar;
import org.junit.Test;
import ddd.logic.Slot;
import ddd.logic.Snack;
import ddd.logic.SnackMachine;
public class SnackMachineTest {
    @Test
    public void
buySnack_trades_inserted_money_for_a_snac
k() {
```

```
        SnackMachine snackMachine = new
SnackMachine();
        snackMachine.loadSnacks(1, new
Snack("Some snack"), 10, 1);
        snackMachine.insertMoney(Dollar);
        snackMachine.buySnack(1);
        assertEquals(snackMachine.getMone
yInTransaction(), 0);
        assertEquals(snackMachine.getMone
yInside().getAmount(), 1, 0.5);
        Slot slot =
snackMachine.getSlots().stream().filter(x ->
x.getPosition() == 1).findAny().orElse(null);
        assertEquals(slot.getQuantity(), 9);
    }
}
```

To overcome the problem, we could create a method that returns a number of snacks in a particular slot. For example, snackMachine.getQuantityOfSnacksInSlot(1) and compare it to the expected value that is 9. This design decision entails other problems, however. If we need to get not only the quantity of the snacks inside a slot, but also the snack itself and its price, we would need to create two other methods, getSnackInSlot and getPriceInSlot, and use them to fetch different pieces of information about the slots. The issue here is that if we need to get a list of all snacks in all slots, those methods would be pretty cumbersome to use. So, how can we overcome this problem? As we discussed before, if our code is hard to use or looks awkward, that is a strong sign we missed some important abstraction. Let's look at the Slot class again. Do you see an abstraction here that we can extract out of this class? It turns out there is one. These three properties, Snack, Quantity, and Price, are always used together, so we can extract them into a separate value object. It makes a lot of sense if you consider the usage scenarios for them in our domain model. In most cases, we want to work with these three elements together. For example, when we display a snack on the interface, we need to know not only what the snack that is, but also its price and the remaining quantity. So let's create a separate class for this new abstraction. We can call it SnackPile. It will represent a pile of snacks a particular slot contains. This would be a value object , remove the setters, because our value object will be immutable. Create a parameter-less constructor, and also a constructor that accepts all three members. Now we can implement the equals and hashCodee methods. We need to add the newly created value object to the Slot entity, and also update its constructor. Here we can just initialize the SnackPile with empty values and remove the snack quantity and price parameters altogether. The SnackMachine class has stopped compiling at this point. Let's see how we can fix it. First of all, the loadSnacks() method doesn't have to accept three separate parameters anymore. We can replace them with a single SnackPile instance and assign that instance to the appropriate slot inside the entity. I need to make the setter for the property public. The constructor of the SnackMachine class can also be simplified. We no longer need to pass any parameters other than SnackMachine itself and the position of the slot. And finally, we have an error here when trying to decrease the number of remaining snacks by one. The first decision that might come to mind is to write such code and just make the quantity field mutable.

126

However, it is not the best solution. Remember, it's a good idea to adhere to the immutability principle, and don't mutate value objects. A better option in this situation is to create a separate method in the ValueObject class, SubtractOne. It would create a new ValueObject with the same parameters as in the existing one, except the quantity value. So let's implement it. We just need to return a new SnackPile with the same snack. The quantity would be decreased by one, and the price is also the same as in the existing ValueObject instance. Perfect.

```
package ddd.logic;
public class SnackPile extends
ValueObject<SnackPile> {
    private Snack snack;
    private int quantity;
    private float price;
    private SnackPile() {
    }
    public SnackPile(Snack snack, int
quantity, float price) {
        this.snack = snack;
        this.quantity = quantity;
        this.price = price;
    }
    public SnackPile subtractOne() {
        return new SnackPile(snack,
getQuantity() - 1, getPrice());
    }
    @Override
    protected boolean equalsCore(SnackPile
other) {
        return this.snack == other.snack &&
this.getQuantity() == other.getQuantity()
                && this.getPrice() ==
other.getPrice();
    }
```

```java
@Override
protected int getHashCodeCore() {
    final int prime = 31;
    int result = super.hashCode();
    result = prime * result +
Float.floatToIntBits(price);
    result = prime * result + quantity;
    result = prime * result + ((snack ==
null) ? 0 : snack.hashCode());
    return result;
}
public int getQuantity() {
    return quantity;
}
public float getPrice() {
    return price;
}
public Snack getSnack() {
    return snack;
}
}
package ddd.logic;
public class Slot extends Entity {
    private SnackPile snackPile;
    private SnackMachine snackMachine;
    private int position;
    public Slot() {
    }
    public Slot(SnackMachine snackMachine,
int position) {
        this.snackMachine = snackMachine;
        this.position = position;
        this.snackPile = new SnackPile(null,
0, 0);
    }
    public SnackPile getSnackPile() {
        return snackPile;
    }
```

```java
    public void setSnackPile(SnackPile
snackPile) {
        this.snackPile = snackPile;
    }
    public SnackMachine getSnackMachine()
{
        return snackMachine;
    }
    public void
setSnackMachine(SnackMachine
snackMachine) {
        this.snackMachine = snackMachine;
    }
    public int getPosition() {
        return position;
    }
    public void setPosition(int position) {
        this.position = position;
    }
}
public class SnackMachine extends
AggregateRoot {
    private Money moneyInside;
    private Money moneyInTransaction;
    private List<Slot> slots;

    public SnackMachine() {
        moneyInside = None;
        moneyInTransaction = None;
        slots = new ArrayList<>();
        slots.add(new Slot(this, 1));
        slots.add(new Slot(this, 2));
        slots.add(new Slot(this, 3));
    }

    public void buySnack(int position) {
        Slot slot = slots.stream().filter(x ->
x.getPosition() ==
position).findAny().orElse(null);
```

```
        slot.setSnackPile(slot.getSnackPile().
subtractOne());
        moneyInside =
Money.add(moneyInside,
moneyInTransaction);
        moneyInTransaction = None;
    }


    public void loadSnacks(int position,
SnackPile snackPile) {
        Slot slot = slots.stream().filter(x ->
x.getPosition() ==
position).findAny().orElse(null);
        if(slot != null) {
            slot.setSnackPile(snackPile);
        }
    }
// rest codes are same as above snack machine
class
}
```

The last thing we need to update is the unit test. Creating a SnackPile to load into the machine and we can create a method that returns a SnackPile from a particular slot. Searching for a slot, and returning its property.

We add this method to SnachMachine class :

```
public SnackPile getSnackPile(int position) {
        return slots.stream().filter(x ->
x.getPosition() ==
position).findAny().orElse(null).getSnackPile()
;
    }
```

Now we can retrieve a SnackPile and check that the quantity in it equals the expected value, and I remove this code. The code compiles and the test is passing now.

```
public class SnackMachineTest {
    @Test
```

```java
    public void
buySnack_trades_inserted_money_for_a_snac
k() {
        SnackMachine snackMachine = new
SnackMachine();
        snackMachine.loadSnacks(1, new
SnackPile(new Snack("Some snack"), 10, 1));
        snackMachine.insertMoney(Dollar);
        snackMachine.buySnack(1);
    assertEquals(snackMachine.getMoneyIn
Transaction(), 0);
assertEquals(snackMachine.getMoneyInside()
.getAmount(), 1, 0.5);
    assertEquals(snackMachine.getSnackPile
(1).getQuantity(), 1);
    }
}
```

Let's implement a couple of additional refactorings for our domain classes.. First, we use "slots.stream().filter(x -> x.getPosition() == position).findAny().orElse(null)" snackmachine class code of getSnachPile() line of code for several times in different methods, so it's a good idea to extract it into a separate method. I call this method getSlot and copy the line to it. Now we can use it.

```java
public class SnackMachine extends
AggregateRoot {
    public Slot getSlot(int position) {
        return slots.stream().filter(x ->
x.getPosition() ==
position).findAny().orElse(null);
    }
    public SnackPile getSnackPile(int
position) {
        return
getSlot(position).getSnackPile();
    }
    public void buySnack(int position) {
```

```
        Slot slot = getSlot(position);
        slot.setSnackPile(slot.getSnackPile().
subtractOne());
      moneyInside =
Money.add(moneyInside,
moneyInTransaction);
      moneyInTransaction = None;
  }
//rest are same
}
```

The last thing you might have noticed is that we don't actually make any validations in the SnackPile ValueObject. It's possible for us to create a pile with a negative quantity or a negative price, which are invalid values for our domain. Let's fix that. If the quantity or price is less than 0, then we throw an exception.

```
public class SnackPile extends
ValueObject<SnackPile> {
    public SnackPile(Snack snack, int
quantity, float price) {
        if (quantity < 0)
            throw new
IllegalStateException();
        if (price < 0)
            throw new
IllegalStateException();
        this.snack = snack;
        this.quantity = quantity;
        this.price = price;
  }
//rest are same
}
```

Note that it's a good idea to cover these two invalid cases with unit tests. I'll leave it as an exercise.

Recap: Refactoring the Snack Machine Aggregate

- Fully encapsulated aggregate
- Not exposing internal Slot entity
- Exposing SnackPilevalue object instead
- New abstraction to resolve the awkwardness

Let's recap what we've done in the previouly. First of all, we created a fully encapsulated aggregate, SnackMachine, that doesn't expose its internals to other aggregates. Not only do we hide the collection of the slots, but we also keep the internal entity, the Slot entity, inside the aggregate and don't expose it to the outside world. It's a good practice to try to achieve such a degree of isolation. In our case, we were able to implement it by introducing a new value object, SnackPile. Unlike entities, value objects are perfectly fine to pass between aggregates. Note how we resolved an awkwardness in the code by adding a new abstraction. Always search for hidden abstractions in your code base. It might be that your domain model can be simplified greatly if you introduce one. And again, unlike entities, value objects are lightweight, and it's always a good idea to move as much domain logic to them as possible. In our case, we transferred almost all responsibilities the slot entity had to the SnackPile value object. The Slot class now acts just as a host for that value object, nothing more. Also note that we adhere to the immutability rule for value objects. Instead of making the quantity property in the SnackPile ValueObject mutable, we introduced a separate method that creates a new instance of that value object.

```
public SnackPile subtractOne() {
    return new SnackPile(snack,
getQuantity() - 1, getPrice());
}
```

Implementing Missing Requirements

- Inserted money is sufficient
- Snack pile is not empty
- Return the change
- The amount of money inside is sufficient to return the change
- Retain small coins and notes

Despite our progress with the domain model, we still have some missing requirements left. First, we need to check if the price of the snack the user is buying is equal to or less than the money they inserted. We shouldn't allow the purchase if it's not the case. Similarly, we must check if there are any snacks left in the slot. Next, we need to return the change back if the user inserts more money than needed, and finally, we shouldn't allow the purchase if there is not enough change in the machine to give the user back. Let's start with the first two requirements, as they are pretty simple to implement. I am adding a test that verifies we cannot make a purchase if there are no snacks in the slot.

```
public class SnackMachineTest {
    @Test(expected =
IllegalStateException.class)
```

```
        public void
cannot_make_purchase_when_there_is_no_sn
acks(){
        SnackMachine snackMachine = new
SnackMachine();
    snackMachine.buySnack(1);
    }
}
```

You can see it just creates an empty snack machine and tries to buy a snack from the first slot. It should fail, because at this point, there are no snacks inside the machine yet. Note that the test is passing. That's because in buySnack() method, we try to create a snack pile by decrementing the quantity of the already existing pile, which essentially gives us a negative number. This number, then, doesn't pass this check. The constructor throws an exception, so we already have the behavior we need. The second test we need to add is the one that verifies that we cannot make a purchase if there is not enough money inserted.

```
@Test(expected = IllegalStateException.class)
        public void
cannot_make_purchase_if_not_enough_mone
y_inserted() {
        SnackMachine snackMachine = new
SnackMachine();
        snackMachine.loadSnacks(1, new
SnackPile(new Snack("Some snack"), 1, 2));
        snackMachine.insertMoney(Dollar);
        snackMachine.buySnack(1);
}
```

So, basically what the test does is it loads the snack with the price two dollars, inserts a dollar, and tries to buy that snack. The test fails, because right now nothing prevents us from buying a snack, even if we don't have enough money in transaction. Let's fix that.

```java
public class SnackMachine extends
AggregateRoot {
    public void buySnack(int position) {
        Slot slot = getSlot(position);
        if(slot.getSnackPile().getPrice() >
moneyInTransaction.getAmount()) {
            throw new
IllegalStateException();
        }
        slot.setSnackPile(slot.getSnackPile().
subtractOne());
        moneyInside =
Money.add(moneyInside,
moneyInTransaction);
        moneyInTransaction = None;
    }
//rest code is same
}
```

So, if the price of the snack in the slot is more than the amount of money in transaction, then we throw an exception. The test passes. Perfect.

Revealing a Hidden Requirement

The next requirement is not as simple as it might seem. We need to make sure the machine returns change, so basically what we need to do is we need to add to the money inside, only the money that is worth the snack price, not more. Right now we just move all inserted money to the money inside, regardless of the snack price. This seemingly simple task raises an important question. What exact set of coins should we transfer? For example, what if the user inserts four quarters and one dollar bill and tries to buy a snack with the price one dollar? Should we transfer quarters, or should it be one dollar bill instead, or maybe it doesn't matter? As always, when we encounter an edge case we didn't think of, we need to go to the domain expert and ask her about the expected behavior. It turns out that this question is more complex than we initially thought, and we have to another business rule to our requirements. That is, the snack machine must try to retain coins and notes of as little denomination as possible. So, in the example above, the machine needs to appropriate four quarters and return the user one dollar bill. That makes sense, because otherwise the machine will run out of change very quickly and won't be able to serve clients who don't have the exact amount of money in hand to make a purchase. It also means that when the user inserts, for example, four quarters, and asks to return the money back, the machine must try to return one dollar bill instead and keep the quarters. All right, let's start with a new test for the ReturnMoney method. The SnackMachine should return the money of the highest denomination first.

```
@Test
    public void
snack_machine_returns_money_with_highest
_denomination_first() {
    SnackMachine snackMachine = new
SnackMachine();
    snackMachine.loadMoney(Dollar);
    snackMachine.insertMoney(Quarter);
    snackMachine.insertMoney(Quarter);
    snackMachine.insertMoney(Quarter);
    snackMachine.insertMoney(Quarter);
    snackMachine.returnMoney();
```

```
assertEquals(snackMachine.getMoneyInside()
.getQuarterCount(), 4);
 assertEquals(snackMachine.getMoneyInside(
).getOneDollarCount() ,0);
   }
```

We need a separate method for this test, loadMoney. We will use it to load some initial money into the machine, just as we do with loadSnacks. So here we load a dollar, try to insert four quarters, and return money. The Return method should be implemented in such a way that allows the machine to keep the quarters and give the user one dollar instead. So the number of quarters inside the machine should be 4, and the number of 1 dollar notes should be 0. Implementing the LoadMoney method, it just adds the money to the money inside. Let's look at the current implementation of the SnackMachine class. Note that we have two separate value objects to represent the money inside the machine, and the money inserted by a user. We know now that we don't have to distinguish them, because it may be that the machine returns to the user not the exact same money they inserted, but the equivalent amount from the money inside. Do we need two separate value objects in this case? We don't. We can just keep all money, be it money inside or money in transaction in a single property, and track the amount the user inserted using a simple numeric variable. So, I can change the type of moneyInTransaction property from money to float, that will be that variable. The MoneyInside property will hold all money in the machine regardless of how they got there. I need to fix the code moneyInTransaction = 0; in constructor. In insertMoney method,

138

Instead of placing the inserted coin or note to the MoneyInTransaction property, we need to just increase the amount and put the money directly to the MoneyInside property. Fixing other occurrences. In the BuySnack method, we don't need to transfer the money from one property to the other. They are already there. So all we need to do here is nullify the MoneyInTransaction. This method still works incorrectly, of course, but we'll get back to it later.

```
public class SnackMachine extends
AggregateRoot {
    private Money moneyInside;
    private float moneyInTransaction;
    private List<Slot> slots;

    public SnackMachine() {
        moneyInside = None;
        moneyInTransaction = 0;
        slots = new ArrayList<>();
        slots.add(new Slot(this, 1));
        slots.add(new Slot(this, 2));
        slots.add(new Slot(this, 3));
    }

    public void insertMoney(Money money) {
        Money[] coinsAndNotes = {
Money.Cent, Money.TenCent,
Money.Quarter, Money.Dollar,
Money.FiveDollar,
            Money.TwentyDollar };
        if
(!Arrays.asList(coinsAndNotes).contains(mon
ey))
            throw new
IllegalStateException();
```

```java
            moneyInTransaction =
moneyInTransaction + money.getAmount();
            moneyInside =
moneyInside.add(money);
    }

        public void buySnack(int position) {
            Slot slot = getSlot(position);
            if(slot.getSnackPile().getPrice() >
moneyInTransaction) {
                throw new
IllegalStateException();
            }
            slot.setSnackPile(slot.getSnackPile().
subtractOne());
        moneyInTransaction = 0;
    }

        public void setMoneyInTransaction(float
moneyInTransaction) {
            this.moneyInTransaction =
moneyInTransaction;
        }
        public float getMoneyInTransaction() {
            return moneyInTransaction;
        }
    public void returnMoney() {
        moneyInTransaction = 0;
    }
//rest code are same
}
```

We need to change controller too.

```java
public class SnackMachineController {
    @PutMapping("/{id}/{slotNumber}")
    public void
buySnack(@PathVariable("id") long id,
@PathVariable("slotNumber") int
slotNumber) {
```

```
                SnackMachineDto snackMachineDto
    =
snackMachineRepository.findById(id).orElse(
null);
                SnackMachine snackMachine =
snackMachineDto.convertToSnackMachine();

                snackMachine.buySnack(slotNumbe
r);
                snackMachineRepository.save(snack
Machine.convertToSnackMachineDto());
    }
    }
//rest are same
}
public class SnackMachine extends
AggregateRoot
    public SnackMachineDto
convertToSnackMachineDto() {
                SnackMachineDto snackMachineDto
= new SnackMachineDto();
                snackMachineDto.setId(id);
snackMachineDto.setMoneyInTransaction(mo
neyInTransaction);
                List<SlotDto> slotDtoList = new
ArrayList<>();
                for(Slot slot : slots)
slotDtoList.add(slot.convertToSlotDto());
                snackMachineDto.setSlotDtoList(slot
DtoList);        snackMachineDto.setOneCentC
ount(moneyInside.getOneCentCount());
    snackMachineDto.setTenCentCount(mone
yInside.getTenCentCount());        snackM
achineDto.setQuarterCount(moneyInside.get
QuarterCount());        snackMachineDto.s
etOneDollarCount(moneyInside.getOneDollar
Count());        snackMachineDto.setFiveD
ollarCount(moneyInside.getFiveDollarCount()
```

141

```java
    );          snackMachineDto.setTwentyDollar
Count(moneyInside.getTwentyDollarCount());
        return snackMachineDto;
    }
//rest are same
}
@Entity
public class SnackMachineDto {
    @Id
    @GeneratedValue
    private long id;
    private int oneCentCount;
    private int tenCentCount;
    private int quarterCount;
    private int oneDollarCount;
    private int fiveDollarCount;
    private int twentyDollarCount;
    private float moneyInTransaction;
    @OneToMany(cascade =
CascadeType.ALL, orphanRemoval = true)
    @JoinColumn(name =
"snackMachineId")
    private List<SlotDto> slotDtoList;

    public SnackMachine
convertToSnackMachine() {
        SnackMachine snackMachine = new
SnackMachine();
        snackMachine.setId(id);
        snackMachine.setMoneyInTransacti
on(moneyInTransaction);
        snackMachine.setMoneyInside(new
Money(oneCentCount,tenCentCount,quarter
Count,
    oneDollarCount,fiveDollarCount,twenty
DollarCount));

        List<Slot> slotList = new
ArrayList<>();
```

```java
            for(SlotDto slotDto : slotDtoList) {
                slotList.add(slotDto.convertToSl
ot());
            }
            snackMachine.setSlots(slotList);
            return snackMachine;
        }
//generate getters and setters
}
```

We can see :

```java
@OneToMany(cascade = CascadeType.ALL,
orphanRemoval = true)@JoinColumn(name =
"snackMachineId")
    private List<SlotDto> slotDtoList;
```

This will change the database table structure too.

But Spring boot do all the table creation for us you can see the tables in H2 console.

The test still fails, however, so we need to change the returnMoney method. To make it work, we need to somehow allocate a required sum from the money inside and subtract it from the overall amount. So, basically what we need here is something like this. Allocate the moneyInTransaction amount, which would be the money to return, and subtract it from the money inside. This Allocate method will handle all the logic while deducting the coins and notes of the highest denomination. I'll just copy the implementation here, but keep in mind that this is definitely something that needs to be covered by unit tests, which I'm leaving as an exercise. You can see we start from the most valuable notes and try to fill the required sum with them first, and then fall down to less valuable notes and coins. After that, we'll return the resulting money object. Good. The test is passing.

```java
public class SnackMachine extends
AggregateRoot {
  public void returnMoney() {
        Money moneyToReturn =
moneyInside.allocate(moneyInTransaction);
        moneyInside =
moneyInside.substract(moneyToReturn);
        moneyInTransaction = 0;
    }
}
public class Money extends
ValueObject<Money> {
    public boolean canAllocate(float
amount){
    Money money = allocateCore(amount);
    return money.amount == amount;
  }
  public Money allocate(float amount){
    if (!canAllocate(amount))
       throw new IllegalStateException();
    return allocateCore(amount);
  }
  private Money allocateCore(float amount){
    int twentyDollarCount =
Math.min((int)(amount / 20),
this.twentyDollarCount);
        amount = amount - twentyDollarCount *
20;
        int fiveDollarCount =
Math.min((int)(amount / 5),
this.fiveDollarCount);
        amount = amount - fiveDollarCount * 5;
        int oneDollarCount =
Math.min((int)amount, this.oneDollarCount);
        amount = amount - oneDollarCount;
        int quarterCount =
Math.min((int)(amount / 0.25f),
this.quarterCount);
```

```
        amount = amount - quarterCount *
0.25f;
        int tenCentCount =
Math.min((int)(amount / 0.1f),
this.tenCentCount);
        amount = amount - tenCentCount * 0.1f;
        int oneCentCount =
Math.min((int)(amount / 0.01f),
this.oneCentCount);
        return new Money(
            oneCentCount,
            tenCentCount,
            quarterCount,
            oneDollarCount,
            fiveDollarCount,
            twentyDollarCount);
    }
}
```

The second piece of functionality we need to implement is returning change after a purchase is completed. So, here I load a snack with a half dollar price, and also load 1 dollar using 10 cent coins. After I insert a dollar and buy a snack, the amount of money inside should be 1 and a half dollars, which means that the machine should take the dollar and give 50 cents back.

```
@Test
    public void
after_purchase_change_is_returned() {
        SnackMachine snackMachine = new
SnackMachine();
        snackMachine.loadSnacks(1, new
SnackPile(new Snack("Some snack"), 1,
0.5f));
        snackMachine.loadMoney(new Money(0,
10, 0, 0, 0, 0));
        snackMachine.insertMoney(Dollar);
        snackMachine.buySnack(1);
```

assertEquals(snackMachine.getMoneyInside()
.getAmount(), 1.5, 0);

assertEquals(snackMachine.getMoneyInTrans
action(), 0, 0);
   }
The test is failing. You can see the snack
machine takes all the inserted money
currently. One little thing to make our code
more readable, we can introduce an additional
multiplication method in the Money class and
implement it like this. Basically multiply all
members by the multiplier. And now instead
of using the money constructor, we can write
10 cent multiplied by 10. Much better. To
make the unit test pass, we need to allocate the
difference between the inserted money and the
price of the snack and subtract it from the
money inside.

```
public void buySnack(int position) {
        Slot slot = getSlot(position);
        if(slot.getSnackPile().getPrice() >
moneyInTransaction) {
                throw new
IllegalStateException();
        }
        slot.setSnackPile(slot.getSnackPile().
subtractOne());
        Money change =
moneyInside.allocate(moneyInTransaction -
slot.getSnackPile().getPrice());
        moneyInside =
moneyInside.substract(change);
        moneyInTransaction = 0;
   }
```

The last use case we have to take into account
is when the machine doesn't have enough
change.

146

```java
@Test(expected = IllegalStateException.class)
    public void
cannot_buy_snack_if_not_enough_change() {
        SnackMachine snackMachine = new
SnackMachine();
    snackMachine.loadSnacks(1, new
SnackPile(new Snack("Some snack"), 1,
0.5f));
    snackMachine.insertMoney(Dollar);
    snackMachine.buySnack(1);
    }
```

You can see the snack costs half a dollar, but
we insert a whole dollar here. That should
result in an exception. To make it work, we
need to check if the change we allocate in is
indeed sufficient. If it's not, the method has to
fail.

```java
public void buySnack(int position) {
        Slot slot = getSlot(position);
        if(slot.getSnackPile().getPrice() >
moneyInTransaction) {
                throw new
IllegalStateException();
        }
        slot.setSnackPile(slot.getSnackPile().
subtractOne());
        Money change =
moneyInside.allocate(moneyInTransaction -
slot.getSnackPile().getPrice());
        if(change.getAmount()<moneyInTra
nsaction - slot.getSnackPile().getPrice()) {
                throw new
IllegalStateException();
        }
        moneyInside =
moneyInside.substract(change);
    moneyInTransaction = 0;
    }
```

Recap: Revealing a Hidden Requirement

Previously, you saw how a new requirement we didn't think of emerged. There almost always will be requirements which you miss initially and which you discover as you progress with your software. It is typical in any more or less complex project. Don't hesitate to refactor a domain model in such situations to make it better convey new knowledge you unfold. It is important to closely collaborate with the domain experts on the new information and try and refine the domain model to the other. In our case, the new requirement let to the situation where we don't have to distinguish the money inside the machine from the money in transaction. It is easy to treat them as a single value object and just drag the amount of money inserted by the user with a decimal property.

Summary

- Aggregates gather multiple entities under a single abstraction
  - Conceptual whole
  - Root entity
  - Single operational unit for the application layer
  - Consistency boundaries
- How to find proper boundaries for aggregates

- Does an entity makes sense by its own?
- Try not to expose internal entities outside the aggregate
- Revealing a hidden abstraction

In this module, we talked about aggregates. That is, a design pattern that stands for gathering multiple entities under a single abstraction. There are several attributes that belong to aggregates. First, an aggregate is a conceptual whole, meaning that they represent a cohesive notion of the domain model. Every aggregate has a set of invariants which it maintains during its lifetime. Second, every aggregate should have a root entity, the root entry, which can be used by other aggregates. All entities and value objects outside a given aggregate should work with it only via its root entity. Third, aggregates act as a single operational unit for the application layer. It means that the application code should work with all aggregates, not with separate entities in it. And finally, aggregates hold consistency boundaries. They should be stored to the database within a single transaction. We talked about how to find proper boundaries for aggregates in your domain model. The best way to do this is to answer question whether or not an entity makes sense as a separate concept. If so, it should be the root of its own aggregate. It's a good idea not to expose internal entities outside of the aggregate boundaries, because it helps maintain proper encapsulation. It's not always possible, but in many cases, it is. And finally, you saw an example of refactoring the domain model after revealing a hidden requirement. Remember there always will be things that you cannot foresee up front. It's important to iteratively involve your domain model after the knowledge you get about the problem you are working on. All right, that's it for this module. In the next one, we will talk about repositories and their connection with aggregates.

Module 5: Introducing Repositories

Introduction

In this module, we will talk about repositories. We will see how they are applicable to our project and what the best practices for working with them are.

Adjusting the Database for the New Entities

In the previous module, we defined two aggregates and added two new entities, snacks and slots. Now let's adjust our database structure by adding new tables for them. This is our domain model.

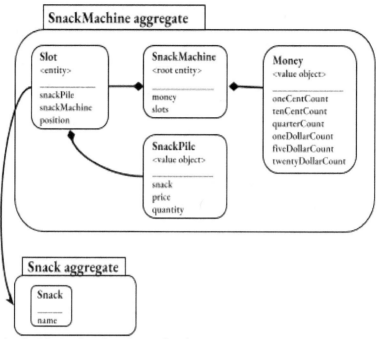

And this is the database for it.

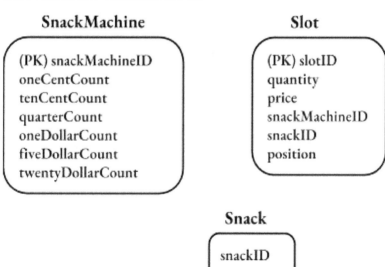

You can see that just as we have the
SnackMachine table, the SnackPile value
object is inline into the Slot table, so that we
don't have a separate table for it.

Repositories

Application service ◄──▷ Repository ◄──▷ Databa

That brings us to another important DDD notion, repository. Repository is a pattern for encapsulating all communications with the database. The idea is that the client code should get the required domain object as if they reside in the memory, just by calling a single method, and without any additional effort. So in our case, a code that retrieves a snack machine could look like this.

```
package ddd.logic.snackMachine;
import
org.springframework.data.repository.CrudRepository;
public interface SnackMachineRepository
extends CrudRepository<SnackMachineDto,
Long> {
}
```

We do not need to implement this interface as Spring Boot will do it for us.

```
SnackMachineDto snackMachineDto =
snackMachineRepository.findById(id).orElse(
null);
```

An important question here is how many repositories should one create for a domain model? The general rule is that there should be a repository per each aggregate.

- one repository per each aggregate

So, in our case, there should be two of them, a SnackMachineRepository and the SnackRepository.

- Repository public methods should
accept and return aggregate roots only

The SnackMachineRepository handles all the
work for retrieving the internal slot instances,
so when we call the code above, not only
should it get the snack machine itself, but also
all its slots. This is usually achieved either by
eagerly the loading the sub-entities with the
aggregate root, or by employing lazy loading.
Similarly, when we save an updated snack
machine, its sub-entities should be saved with
it without additional effort from outside.
Another rule of thumb for working with
repositories is that the public methods should
work with aggregate roots only. The
SnackMachineRepository should accept and
return the SnackMachine instances. All the
work with internal entities has to be done
behind the scenes, either manually in the
repository, or using ORM mapping
capabilities. At this point, you might ask, what
if you need to get a sub-entity instance? What
if you don't know to each parent the sub-
entity instance belongs? A common practice in
this case is retrieving an aggregate root
instance first, and working with it to get the
required sub-entity. For example, in our case,
if the client code would like to retrieve a slot
by its identifier, we could create a method like
this one.

Repository repository = new
SnackMachineRepository();
SnackMachine snackMachine =
repository.getBySlotId(slotId);

You can see this method resides in the
SnackMachineRepository, and although it
accepts a slotId, it returns an instance of
SnackMachine, not Slot. Aside from utilizing
an ORM, repositories can work with the

database directly, either by using SQL or by calling stored procedures. So, it's a good idea to commission all communications with the database to repositories, even if such communications bypass the ORM. An example here would be reading a list of Snackmachines and sending it to the client. If such query is performance sensitive, you can write a separate SQL script for it and use it from the repository directly without involving the ORM and domain objects. We will talk about this approach in more detail in the future modules.

Setting up Mappings for the Aggregates

Now, as we have repositories in place, let's discuss the mapping for the new domain entities. This is a mapping for the Snack class.

```java
package ddd.logic;
import javax.persistence.Entity;
import javax.persistence.Id;
@Entity
public class SnackDto {
    @Id
    private long id;
    private String name;
    public long getId() {
        return id;
    }
    public void setId(long id) {
        this.id = id;
    }
    public String getName() {
        return name;
```

```java
    }
    public void setName(String name) {
        this.name = name;
    }

    public Snack convertToSnack() {
        if(id==0) return Snack.None;
        else if(id==1) return
Snack.Chocolate;
        else if(id==2) return Snack.Soda;
        else return Snack.Gum;
    }
}
```

This class is very simple, so is the mapping for it. All it contains is the ID and the Name properties. The slot mapping is a little bit more complex.

```java
package ddd.logic;
@Entity
public class SlotDto {
    @Id
    @GeneratedValue
    private long id;
    private int quantity;
    private float price;
    @OneToOne(cascade =
CascadeType.ALL)
    private SnackDto snackDto;
    private int position;
    public long getId() {
        return id;
    }
    public void setId(long id) {
        this.id = id;
    }
    public int getQuantity() {
        return quantity;
    }
    public void setQuantity(int quantity) {
```

```java
        this.quantity = quantity;
    }
    public float getPrice() {
        return price;
    }
    public void setPrice(float price) {
        this.price = price;
    }
    public SnackDto getSnackDto() {
        return snackDto;
    }
    public void setSnackDto(SnackDto
snackDto) {
        this.snackDto = snackDto;
    }
    public int getPosition() {
        return position;
    }
    public void setPosition(int position) {
        this.position = position;
    }
    public Slot convertToSlot() {
        Slot slot = new Slot();
        slot.setId(id);
        slot.setPosition(position);
        slot.setSnackPile(new
SnackPile(snackDto.convertToSnack(),
quantity, price));
        return slot;
    }
}
package ddd.logic;
@Entity
public class SnackMachineDto {
    @Id
    @GeneratedValue
    private long id;
    private int oneCentCount;
    private int tenCentCount;
```

```java
    private int quarterCount;
    private int oneDollarCount;
    private int fiveDollarCount;
    private int twentyDollarCount;
    private float moneyInTransaction;
    @OneToMany(cascade =
CascadeType.ALL, orphanRemoval = true)
    @JoinColumn(name =
"snackMachineId")
    private List<SlotDto> slotDtoList;
    @Transient
    private float amount ;
    public float getAmount() {
        return  amount;
    }
    @PostLoad
    public void setAmount() {
        amount = oneCentCount * 0.01f +
tenCentCount * 0.10f + quarterCount * 0.25f
+ oneDollarCount * 1f
                    + fiveDollarCount * 5f +
twentyDollarCount * 20f;
    }
    public SnackMachine
convertToSnackMachine() {
        SnackMachine snackMachine = new
SnackMachine();
        snackMachine.setId(id);
        snackMachine.setMoneyInTransacti
on(moneyInTransaction);
        snackMachine.setMoneyInside(new
Money(oneCentCount,tenCentCount,quarter
Count,
                    oneDollarCount,fiveDollar
Count,twentyDollarCount));

        List<Slot> slotList = new
ArrayList<>();
        for(SlotDto slotDto : slotDtoList) {
```

```
                    slotList.add(slotDto.convertToSl
ot());
            }
            snackMachine.setSlots(slotList);
            return snackMachine;
    }
// generate getters and setters for all fields

}
```
Now if we restart our application Spring boot will creat all the tables for us.

Refactoring the Snack Entity

Let's look at the snack table again. It turns out that in our domain model, the list of snacks is reference data. Reference data is data that is pre-defined. The change of such data is relatively rare and we can treat it the same way we treat the database structure. Another example of reference data is the Id table. We add new rows to it only when the database structure is changed. The users don't minify those rows directly. Reference data enables some interest in approach we can leverage in our domain model. Our code can rely on the existence of those snacks in the database, and we can define them explicitly. Let's see what I mean by that. Here's the Snack class. You can see that whenever we need a new instance of it, we'll create one via the constructor, like this. What we can do instead is we can add an Id parameter, make the constructor private, and add a static readonly field, Chocolate, by creating a snack with the same data as in the database. And the same for the other two snacks. And note that the constructor is made private, so these read-only fields is the only way for the client code to work with the instances of the Snack class. You can see they fully represent the data in the database.

```java
package ddd.logic;
public class Snack extends AggregateRoot {
    public static Snack Chocolate = new Snack(1, "Chocolate");
    public static Snack Soda = new Snack(2, "Soda");
    public static Snack Gum = new Snack(3, "Gum");
    private String name;
    private Snack(long id, String name) {
        this.id = id;
        this.name = name;
    }
    public SnackDto convertToSnackDto() {
        SnackDto snackDto = new SnackDto();
        snackDto.setId(id);
        snackDto.setName(name);
        return snackDto;
    }
}
```

It's a good practice to also cover them with integration tests to make sure the ID and the name you set up in the domain model are the same as in the database. Now as we've defined the existing snacks in the declarative manner, we can replace this explicit snack instantiation with a read-only field. Even more, we can also define it as a static import just as we did with the Money class. That would allow us to shorten the invocation.

In SnackMachineTest.java

Replace all " new Snack("Some snack") "
with " Chocolate "
There are several more places where I need to
update it. Perfect. And let's also look at the
Slot class. You can see the constructor
instantiates the SnackPile, passing it null as
the snack instance. A better way to deal with
such situations is to employ the null value
design pattern. This pattern stands for the use
of some special value instead of null. We can
define it here along with the other snacks
we've declared.

```
public class Snack extends AggregateRoot {
    public static Snack None = new Snack(0,
"None");
//rest are same
}
```

The benefit of this pattern is that it decreases
the chance of incorrect behavior that can
appear because of nulls. And it's a good idea
to cover this field with an integration test as
well, but at this time, the test should check
that this field does not exist in the database.
So, after we created a null object, we can use it
here instead of null.

```
public class Slot extends Entity {
    public Slot(SnackMachine snackMachine,
int position) {
        this.snackMachine = snackMachine;
        this.position = position;
        this.snackPile = new
SnackPile(Snack.None, 0, 0);
    }
//rest are same
}
```

But we can do even better. Just as we've
defined a null object for the snack entity, we
can define one for the SnackPile value object
and use it for initializing newly created slots.

```java
public class SnackPile extends
ValueObject<SnackPile> {
    public static SnackPile Empty = new
SnackPile(Snack.None, 0, 0f);
//rest are same
}
public class Slot extends Entity {
    public Slot(SnackMachine snackMachine,
int position) {
        this.snackMachine = snackMachine;
        this.position = position;
        this.snackPile = SnackPile.Empty;
    }
    public SlotDto convertToSlotDto() {
        SlotDto slotDto = new SlotDto();
        slotDto.setId(id);
        slotDto.setPosition(position);
        slotDto.setPrice(snackPile.getPrice())
;
        slotDto.setQuantity(snackPile.getQu
antity());
        slotDto.setSnackDto(snackPile.getSn
ack().convertToSnackDto());
        return slotDto;
    }
//rest are same
}
```
This is a quite powerful technique, and it can significantly simplify your code base. An important note here is that you shouldn't forget to change those values every time you change the reference data. Because of that, it is vital to cover the static fields with integration tests to verify they match the data in the database.

Adjusting Project for User Interface

Chocolate price:$ Soda price:$ Gum price:$

Chocolate quantity: Soda quantity: Gum quantity:

[Buy a Chocolate]   [Buy a Soda]   [Buy a Gum]

Money inserted :$

[Insert 1 cent coin]   [Insert 10 cent coin]   [Insert 25 cent coin]

[Insert 1 dollar note]   [Insert 5 dollar note]   [Insert 20 dollar note]

[Return Money]

No of coins and notes in Snack machine :

No. of 1 cent coin :   No. of 10 cent coin :   No. of 25 cent coin :

No. of 1 dollar note :   No. of 5 dollar note :   No. of 20 dollar note

SnackMachineView.html :
<!DOCTYPE html>
<html>
<body>
**   <table style="width:100%">**
**   <tr>**
**   <td><span>Chocolate**
price:$<span
id="chocolatePrice"></span></span></td>
**   <td><span>Soda price:$<span**
id="sodaPrice"></span></span></td>
**   <td><span>Gum price:$<span**
id="gumPrice"></span></span></td>
**   </tr>**
**   <tr>**

```html
          <td><span>Chocolate
quantity:<span
id="chocolateQuantity"></span></span></td
>
          <td><span>Soda
quantity:<span
id="sodaQuantity"></span></span></td>
          <td><span>Gum
quantity:<span
id="gumQuantity"></span></span></td>
      </tr>
      <tr>
          <td><button
id="btnBuyChocolate">Buy a Chocolate</td>
          <td><button
id="btnBuySoda">Buy a Soda</td>
          <td><button
id="btnBuyGum">Buy a Gum</td>
      </tr>
      <tr>
  </table>
  </br>
  </br>
  </br>
  <span>Money inserted :$<span
id="moneyInserted"></span></span>
  </br>
  <table style="width:100%">
      </tr>
      <td><button
id="btnInsertCent">Insert 1 cent
coin</button></td>
      <td><button
id="btnInsertTenCent">Insert 10 cent
coin</button></td>
      <td><button
id="btnInsertQuarter">Insert 25 cent
coin</button></td>
      </tr>
```

```html
    </tr>
    <td><button
id="btnInsertDollar">Insert 1 dollar
note</button></td>
    <td><button
id="btnInsertFiveDollar">Insert 5 dollar
note</button></td>
    <td><button
id="btnInsertTwentyDollar">Insert 20 dollar
        note</button></td>
    </tr>
    </table>
    </br>
    </br>
    <button id="btnReturnMoney">Return
Money</button>
    </br>
    </br>
    </br>
    <div>No of coins and notes in Snack
machine :</div>
    <table style="width:100%">
        </tr>
        <td>No. of 1 cent coin : <span
id="cent"></span></td>
        <td>No. of 10 cent coin : <span
id="tenCent"></span> </td>
        <td>No. of 25 cent coin : <span
id="quarter"></span> </td>
        </tr>

        </tr>
        <td>No. of 1 dollar note : <span
id="dollar"></span></td>
        <td>No. of 5 dollar note : <span
id="fiveDollar"></span></td>
        <td>No. of 20 dollar note : <span
id="twentyDollar"></span></td>
        </tr>
```

```
        </table>
        <script src="../common/jquery-
3.3.1.js"></script>
        <script src="snackMachine.js"></script>
</body>
</html>
```

snackMachine.js :

```
let searchParams = new
URLSearchParams(window.location.search)
let param = '';
if(searchParams.has('id')){
    param = searchParams.get('id')
}else{
    param='1';
}
const rootURI =
"http://localhost:8080/snackmachines/"+para
m;
getSnachMachine();
function getSnachMachine(){
    $.get(rootURI, function(data, status){
        $('#moneyInserted').html(data.mone
yInTransaction);
        $('#chocolatePrice').html(data.slotDt
oList[0].price);
        $('#sodaPrice').html(data.slotDtoList
[1].price);
        $('#gumPrice').html(data.slotDtoList
[2].price);
        $('#chocolateQuantity').html(data.sl
otDtoList[0].quantity);
        $('#sodaQuantity').html(data.slotDto
List[1].quantity);
        $('#gumQuantity').html(data.slotDto
List[2].quantity);

        $('#cent').html(data.oneCentCount);
        $('#tenCent').html(data.tenCentCou
nt);
```

```
            $('#quarter').html(data.quarterCoun
t);
            $('#dollar').html(data.oneDollarCou
nt);
            $('#fiveDollar').html(data.fiveDollar
Count);
            $('#twentyDollar').html(data.twenty
DollarCount);

   });
}
$("button").click(function() {
   switch (this.id) {
   case "btnInsertCent" :
       insert("Cent")
     break;
   case "btnInsertTenCent" :
       insert("TenCent")
     break;
   case "btnInsertQuarter" :
       insert("Quarter")
     break;
   case "btnInsertDollar" :
       insert("Dollar")
     break;
   case "btnInsertFiveDollar" :
       insert("FiveDollar")
     break;
   case "btnInsertTwentyDollar" :
       insert("TwentyDollar")
     break;
   case "btnReturnMoney" :
       returnMoney()
     break;
   case "btnBuyChocolate" :
       buy("1")
     break;
   case "btnBuySoda" :
       buy("2")
```

```
          break;
       case "btnBuyGum" :
             buy("3")
          break;
       default :
          break;
}
});
function insert(coinOrNote){
    $.ajax({
       url:
rootURI+'/moneyInTransaction/'+coinOrNote
,
       type: 'PUT',
       success: function(result) {
          // Do something with the result
       }
    });
    location.reload();
}
function returnMoney(){
    $.ajax({
       url: rootURI+'/moneyInTransaction',
       type: 'PUT',
       success: function(result) {
          // Do something with the result
       }
    });
    location.reload();
}
function buy(position){
    $.ajax({
       url: rootURI+'/'+position,
       type: 'PUT',
       success: function(result) {
          // Do something with the result
       }
    });
    location.reload();
```

```
}
```

SnackMachineController.java :
```
package ddd.logic.snackMachine;
import
org.springframework.beans.factory.annotatio
n.Autowired;
import
org.springframework.stereotype.Controller;
import
org.springframework.web.bind.annotation.Ge
tMapping;
import
org.springframework.web.bind.annotation.Pat
hVariable;
import
org.springframework.web.bind.annotation.Po
stMapping;
import
org.springframework.web.bind.annotation.Pu
tMapping;
import
org.springframework.web.bind.annotation.Re
questMapping;
import
org.springframework.web.bind.annotation.Re
sponseBody;
import static
ddd.logic.sharedKernel.Money.Cent;
import static
ddd.logic.sharedKernel.Money.TenCent;
import static
ddd.logic.sharedKernel.Money.Quarter;
import static
ddd.logic.sharedKernel.Money.Dollar;
import static
ddd.logic.sharedKernel.Money.FiveDollar;
import static
ddd.logic.sharedKernel.Money.TwentyDollar;
import java.util.ArrayList;
```

```java
import java.util.List;
import
ddd.logic.snackMachine.SnackMachine;
import
ddd.logic.snackMachine.SnackMachineReposi
tory;
@Controller
@RequestMapping(path = "/snackmachines")
public class SnackMachineController {
    @Autowired
    SnackMachineRepository
snackMachineRepository;
    @GetMapping()
    @ResponseBody
    public List<SnackMachineDto>
getSnackMachines() {
    List<SnackMachineDto> list = new
ArrayList<>();

snackMachineRepository.findAll().forEach(lis
t::add);
    return list;
    }

    @GetMapping("/{id}")
    @ResponseBody
    public SnackMachineDto
getSnackMachine(@PathVariable("id") long
id) {
    return
snackMachineRepository.findById(id).orElse(
null);
    }
    @PutMapping("/{id}/{slotNumber}")
    public void
buySnack(@PathVariable("id") long id,
@PathVariable("slotNumber") int
slotNumber) {
```

```java
        SnackMachineDto snackMachineDto
=
snackMachineRepository.findById(id).orElse(
null);
        SnackMachine snackMachine =
snackMachineDto.convertToSnackMachine();

        snackMachine.buySnack(slotNumbe
r);
        snackMachineRepository.save(snack
Machine.convertToSnackMachineDto());
    }

    @PutMapping("/{id}/moneyInTransactio
n/{coinOrNote}")
    public void
insertCoinOrNote(@PathVariable("id") long
id, @PathVariable("coinOrNote") String
coinOrNote) {
        SnackMachineDto snackMachineDto
=
snackMachineRepository.findById(id).orElse(
null);
        SnackMachine snackMachine =
snackMachineDto.convertToSnackMachine();

        if(coinOrNote.equalsIgnoreCase("Ce
nt")) snackMachine.insertMoney(Cent);
        else
if(coinOrNote.equalsIgnoreCase("TenCent"))
snackMachine.insertMoney(TenCent);
        else
if(coinOrNote.equalsIgnoreCase("Quarter"))
snackMachine.insertMoney(Quarter);
        else
if(coinOrNote.equalsIgnoreCase("Dollar"))
snackMachine.insertMoney(Dollar);
```

```
        else
if(coinOrNote.equalsIgnoreCase("FiveDollar"
)) snackMachine.insertMoney(FiveDollar);
        else
if(coinOrNote.equalsIgnoreCase("TwentyDoll
ar"))
snackMachine.insertMoney(TwentyDollar);

        snackMachineRepository.save(snack
Machine.convertToSnackMachineDto());
    }
    @PutMapping("/{id}/moneyInTransactio
n")
    public void
returnMoney(@PathVariable("id") long id) {
        SnackMachineDto snackMachineDto
=
snackMachineRepository.findById(id).orElse(
null);
        SnackMachine snackMachine =
snackMachineDto.convertToSnackMachine();

        snackMachine.returnMoney();
        snackMachineRepository.save(snack
Machine.convertToSnackMachineDto());
    }
}
```

Summary

- **Repositories encapsulate all communication with the external storage**
    - **Single repository per each aggregate**

- Public API works with aggregate roots only
- Perform persistence of sub-entities behind the scenes
- Define reference data in your domain model explicitly

In this module, we talked about repositories. Repository is a pattern the purpose of which is to encapsulate all communication with external storage. It's important to keep in mind a general rule of thumb there should be a single repository per each aggregate. Another guideline here is that public methods of repositories work with aggregate roots only. If you need to get a sub-entity, retrieve its aggregate root first, and only after that look among its sub-entities. But keep in mind the guideline we discussed in the previous module. Try not to expose sub-entities outside of aggregates wherever possible. Repositories work with whole aggregates, meaning that they should perform saving and retrieval of all sub-entities without additional effort from the client side. It is best achieved by configuring proper mappings in the ORM. You also saw an example of working with reference data. It's a good practice to declaratively define such data in the domain model. It helps simplify the code and increase its readability. In the next module, we will talk about bounded contexts. We will introduce a second bounded context and we'll discuss different ways to express them in code.

Module 6: Introducing the Second Bounded Context

Introduction

- **Bounded Contexts vs Sub-domains**
- **Boundaries**
- **Context Mapping**
- **Types of isolation**
- **Communication**
- **Code Reuse**

In this module, we'll introduce the second bounded context in our application. Along the way, we'll discuss the differences between bounded contexts and sub-domains, and how they relate to each other. We will also talk about how to choose boundaries for them and how to perform context mapping. We will look at different types of physical isolation for bounded contexts, how they communicate with each other, and finally, we'll discuss the guidelines for using code between them.

New Task: an ATM Model

- **Problem Description :**
  - **Dispense cash**
  - **Charge the user's bank card**
  - **Keep track of all money charged**

In the previous modules, we ended up with a snack machine model. Now we have given a new task. Create another model, and this time for an automated teller machine, ATM. This model will allow the users to withdraw cash using their bank cards. Just as with the snack machine, here we'll leave aside such details as how exactly card operations are performed or how the ATM dispenses cash. Our focus area will be the business rules behind this model. So, what are the requirements for this new task? First of all, the ATM must give the users cash they requested. In return, their bank cards should be charged the worth of money dispensed, plus a 1% fee. Also, the model must keep track of all money that was charged from clients. To solve this task, we'll introduce a new bounded context. We'll discuss the reasons for that shortly. For now, let's take a closer look at the notion of bounded context.

Bounded Contexts

- **Separation of the model into smaller ones**

Bounded context is a central pattern in domain-driven design. It stands for separating the model and explicitly drawing the

174

boundaries between its pieces. The reason for such separation is that as your application grows, it becomes harder to maintain a single unified model as it becomes larger and more people get involved into the development process. Big models bring significant communication and integration overhead with them. Bounded contexts help reduce that overhead. There are several attributes that belong to the notion of bounded contexts.

- Boundary for the ubiquitous language
- Span across all layers in the onion architecture
- Explicit relationships between different bounded contexts

First of all, they act as a boundary for the ubiquitous language. It means that the language we use for communicating with domain experts and naming classes in our domain model should be consistent and unified only within a bounded context. At the same time, the naming doesn't have to be consistent across different models. Two bounded contexts can hold entities or value objects with the same name, and they can be completely unrelated to each other. That's perfectly fine. You can think of bounded contexts as if they were Java package for the classes in your code base. Two packages can hold any set of classes, be they intersecting or not. For example, the SnackMachine bounded context could have a class name CompositeElement, which represents a replaceable item in a machine. The ATM bounded context at the same time could have its own version of that class with its own set of attributes and business rules. These classes, despite the same name, should be viewed

175

differently, as they reflect different concepts. Another important attribute of bounded contexts is that they span across all layers in the onion architecture. Each of them is represented with its own onion (onion architecture). So, if you decide to introduce a new bounded context, it should have its own set of entities, repositories, factories, Application Services, and all other layers from the onion architecture. And finally, it's important to explicitly state the relations between bounded contexts. That's where context maps come into play. A context map is a map that renders the bounded contexts in your system and the connections between them. We will draw our own context map later in this module.

Bounded Contexts and Sub-domains

Sub-domain ⟷ Bounded Context
Problem space   Solution space
1-to-1 relation

There is another concept in domain-driven design, sub-domain. It's important to understand the relation between sub-domains and bounded contexts, as they are often mistaken by programmers. There are two central elements when it comes to building a software project, a problem and a solution. The problem is the reason why we are creating the project, the thing we aim to solve with it. The solution is the actual artifact of our efforts of trying to solve the problem. So, the differences between the two concepts is that sub-domain belongs to the problem space, whereas bounded context to the solution space. In other words, a sub-domain is a part of the whole problem, a part of the problem domain, and bounded contexts at the same time is a part of the solution for that problem. Sub-domains and bounded contexts are best related to each other as 1-to-1, meaning that ideally every sub-domain should be covered by exactly one bounded context. It's not always possible, though.

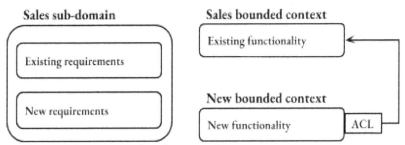

Let's say, for example, that you've come to legacy ERP project, which you need to enhance to address new requirements for the sales sub-domain. If the existing code base isn't covered by automated tests, it might be scary to change it, so you might decide to add a new bounded context and separate it from the existing code base by an anti-corruption layer. In this case, you end up with two bounded contexts that cover a single sale sub-domain. It's a good practice to avoid such situations, though, because the code base is overall easy to maintain and understand where there is a strict 1-to-1 relation between sub-domains and bounded contexts. So, in the example above, there should be ideally a single sales bounded context. In our case, we have two sub-domains, snack machine and ATM.

As we are working on a greenfield project, meaning that we don't have any legacy code here, it's easy for us to adhere to the guideline and create a single bounded context for each sub-domain.

Choosing Boundaries for Bounded Contexts

It's important to keep explicit boundaries between bounded contexts, but how to define them in the first place? How to draw a line between one bounded context and another? As I mentioned earlier, the best way to do that is to adhere to the 1-to-1 guideline. In other words, create a separate bounded context for each sub-domain. So, the question boils down to how to define a sub-domain? A sub-domain is usually not something that is defined by us developers. As the notion of sub-domain refers to the problem space, it is often defined by customers and domain experts. The boundaries for sub-domains usually come up naturally during the talks with them. For example, they might mention that they want to build a sales prediction subsystem to help the company stabilize its revenue. Or they want a support subsystem to decrease the expenses related to the customer support activities. All these are signs of separate sub-domains, so in most situations, you just need to carefully listen to the domain experts. However, this approach might not work in some cases, as you need to take into account other factors as well. The first one is the size of the team. If your sub-domain is too big and that causes the team working on it to grow more than, say, 6-8 developers, it's a strong sign you need to separate the bounded context in 2 and form an independent team for each of them. The second factor is the size of the code. Even if your team was small enough, it might be that the code in a bounded context grows enormously so that it becomes hard to manage its complexity. In this case, you might also want to depart from the 1-to-1 guideline and create 2 bounded contexts for a single sub-domain. The general rule of thumb here is that the code of single bounded context should fit your head, meaning that you shouldn't have a lot of trouble understanding it. In my experience, though, it rarely happens, and the 1-to-1 guideline works just fine in most situations. All right, we discussed situations where there might be several bounded contexts for a single sub-domain, but what about the opposite? Can a single bounded context cover several sub-domains? For example, in our application of the snack machine and ATM sub-domains are pretty small, doesn't it make sense to solve those problems with a single bounded context? It's true that in our sample application, there is little code in bounded contexts. For example, the snack machine model consists of only two aggregates. Nevertheless, even if you are able to cover two sub-domains with a single bounded context and still keep it succinct, I recommend you to adhere to the guideline and still create two separate bounded contexts for them. Just make sure the sub-domains they cover are indeed distinct ones and not part of a single sub-domain. The reason here is that bounded context segregation is a logical one. Whether or not to keep them separated physically is a different question. So, even if you do create two bounded contexts, you don't have to create separate sets of projects for them right away. You can carry the code together while it's small and thus keep the maintenance overhead low. We will talk about the degrees of physical isolation for bounded contexts later in this module. The last guideline regarding boundaries for bounded contexts is how they relate to the development teams working on them. It's a good practice to keep the team's boundaries aligned with those of bounded contexts. It means that while one team may work on several bounded contexts, there shouldn't be a situation where two teams work on a single bounded context. It would lead to communication issues and increased maintenance costs.

Drawing a Context Map

Let's draw a map for the context we have in our application. But before that, let's see how the structure of the ATM bounded context looks like.

Atm

atmMoneyInside : Money
moneyChardged : float

It will consist of a single aggregate with an ATM entity inside. As the ATM needs to dispense cash, we need to represent that cash somehow, and we already have a suitable class for that, MoneyValueObject, which we can use the ATM entity. Another field here is the

MoneyCharged field, which will indicate the amount of money charged from the client's bank cards. So, now we have a situation where the same value object, MoneyValueObject, is used in both bounded contexts. That means there is a shared kernel between them. So, our map goes like this.

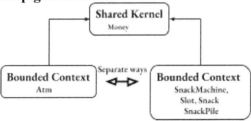

You can see the two bounded contexts use a shared kernel and don't interact with each other. So, we can say there is a separate ways relation between them. That kind of relationship actually indicates no relation, whatsoever. It's important to remember that such maps should reflect the actual state of affairs, not the desired one. If the bounded contexts in the application interfere poorly, for example, one of them has become a big ball of mud and starts affecting other contexts, show it with such diagram. It will be a good starting point on the way to fix the situation. If you see that one of the bounded contexts decays, meaning that the code in it is a mess, you might want to protect other bounded contexts from its impact by introducing an anti-corruption layer.

Types of Physical Isolation

As I mentioned earlier, logical separation of bounded context is orthogonal to the physical isolation. There are several degrees of such isolation you may employ, and each of them has its own pros and cons.

Type 1:

- **Same jars**
- **Shared database instance**

```
∨ 🗁 MyProjectLogic
  ∨ 🍃 src/main/java
    ∨ ⊞ boundedContext1
      > 🗾 Entity1.java
      > 🗾 ValueObject1.java
    ∨ ⊞ boundedContext2
      > 🗾 Entity2.java
      > 🗾 ValueObject2.java
    ∨ ⊞ sharedKernel
      > 🗾 ValueObject3.java

∨ 🗁 MyProjectUI
  ∨ 🍃 src/main/java
    ∨ ⊞ boundedContext1
      > 🗾 View1.java
    ∨ ⊞ boundedContext2
      > 🗾 View2.java
```

The first one is keeping the bounded context in the same jars, but in different packages, so basically just creating separate folders for them. Note that although with this type of isolation you keep the code of the bounded context physically close, you still need to maintain proper separation, and don't allow them to infiltrate to each other. Boundaries should be preserved regardless of what type of isolation is chosen. Such degree of separation also means you share the same database instance, but again, entities in different bounded contexts should be stored in different tables. If you use SQL Server, it's a good idea to define separate database schemas for each bounded context to make this distinction more apparent.

Type 2:

- **Separate jars**

```
v 📁 BoundedContext1
   v 🗁 src/main/java
      v ⊞ boundedContext1Logic
         > 🗋 Entity1.java
         > 🗋 ValueObject1.java
      v ⊞ boundedContext1UI
         > 🗋 View1.java

v 📁 BoundedContext2
   v 🗁 src/main/java
      v ⊞ boundedContext2Logic
         > 🗋 Entity2.java
         > 🗋 ValueObject2.java
      v ⊞ boundedContext2UI
         > 🗋 View2.java

v 📁 SharedKernel
   v 🗁 src/main/java
      v ⊞ (default package)
         > 🗋 ValueObject3.java
```

The second type of isolation is extracting the bounded contexts into separate jars under the same solution. Here, for example, you can see two solution folders for bounded contexts, and a separate project for the SharedKernel. Note that each folder contains its own UI and logic assemblies that regard to certain bounded context.

Type 3:

- **Separate deployments**
- **Run in separate processes**
- **Microservices**

The third type of isolation is separate deployment. While the first two types imply the bounded context work in a single physical process, this type of isolation means you deploy and maintain them as separate applications. The source code is stored separately and there are separate database instances for each of the bounded contexts. This type of isolation is often referred to as microservices. It's important to understand the benefits and drawbacks that each of the isolation types entail.

Type 1   ------>   Type 2   ------->   Type 3

- Easier to maintain proper isolation
- Bigger maintenance overhead

The benefit here is that the greater the physical isolation is, the easier it is to maintain proper boundaries between bounded contexts. You are less likely to violate them if the bounded contexts reside in separate assemblies, or even separate solutions. At the same time, the more you isolate your bounded contexts, the more maintenance overhead this isolation introduces. It's harder to deal with separate assemblies in your code base than it is with only one, and it's even more difficult to handle separate deployment of them in case the third type of isolation is chosen.

- Start with Type 1 isolation
- Move further only if necessary

The guideline here is that you should be pragmatic about the degree of isolation you choose, and introduce greater physical separation only when the benefits of it is justified. If your bounded contexts are small enough, it's just fine to start with the first type and move forward only when you feel the code gets bigger and it becomes harder to keep it clean without introducing additional physical boundaries. In our application, we will adhere to the first type, because we don't have large amounts of code in our bounded contexts. We have one Spring boot project with name "logic" for the domain logic and one Static web project named "UI" containing HTML and JS files only. This is how our logic project look like. Yo can see its project structure in the next page.

- ⌄ logic
  - ⌄ src/main/java
    - ⌄ ddd.logic
      - > LogicApplication.java
    - > ddd.logic.atm
    - ⌄ ddd.logic.common
      - > AggregateRoot.java
      - > Entity.java
      - > Repository.java
      - > ValueObject.java
    - > ddd.logic.management
    - ⌄ ddd.logic.sharedKernel
      - > Money.java
    - ⌄ ddd.logic.snackMachine
      - > Slot.java
      - > SlotDto.java
      - > Snack.java
      - > SnackDto.java
      - > SnackMachine.java
      - > SnackMachineController.java
      - > SnackMachineDto.java
      - > SnackMachineRepository.java
      - > SnackPile.java
    - > ddd.logic.utils
  - > src/main/resources
  - ⌄ src/test/java
    - ⌄ ddd.logic
      - > LogicApplicationTests.java
      - > SnackMachineRepositoryTests.java
      - > SnackMachineTest.java
  - > JRE System Library [JavaSE-1.8]
  - > Project and External Dependencies
  - > bin
  - > gradle
  - > src
  - build.gradle
  - gradlew
  - gradlew.bat
  - settings.gradle
  - snackMachineData.sql

186

Note : Change the package structure of the the previous codes as per the image shown in previous page and fix the import statements accordingly.

Now the second project we have is Static web project named "UI" .

This is the structure shown below.

```
∨ 📚 UI
    > 📚 JavaScript Resources
    ∨ 📂 WebContent
        > 📂 atm
        ∨ 📂 common
            > 📄 jquery-3.3.1.js
        > 📂 headOffice
        ∨ 📂 snackMachine
            > 📄 snackMachine.js
              📄 SnackMachineView.html
          📂 utils
```

You can see there is a separate folder for the snack machine context with all classes related to it. The Atms folder is empty, because we don't have any code for the new bounded context yet. And the SharedKernel contains a single Money value object. Note that we also have a folder for Common base classes, and they are the one for utilities. They are shared by all bounded contexts. We will talk about sharing code between bounded contexts later in this book. Also note that we have the same kind of separation in the UI project, two separate folders for each of the bounded contexts.

Communication Between Bounded Contexts

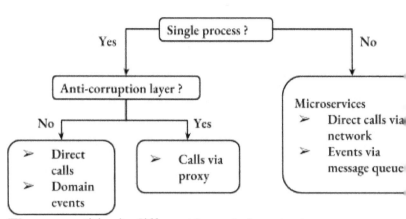

The way entities in different bounded contexts communicate with each other depends on two elements, the type of isolation chosen and the relationship between them. Let's take the first two isolation types, the types that imply you host bounded contexts in a single process. In this case, the communication pattern depends on whether or not there is an anti-corruption layer between the bounded contexts. If there is none, entities in these bounded contexts can just call other entities' methods directly. Also, the communication can be performed via domain events, which we'll discuss in the next module. In case there is an anti-corruption layer, things get more complicated, and anti-corruption layer usually means that developers working on one bounded context don't want to interfere with the concepts from another bounded context. It's often the case if that other bounded context has become a big ball of mud, or in other words, a mess. Another use case for introducing a such a layer is working on the legacy project, where you want to keep the new code isolated from the concepts in the existing code base. Regardless of the actual reason, the presence of an anti-corruption layer means that you cannot just allow entities in your model, call entities from the other bounded context. You need to introduce the proxy between the two models, which would handle all translations for them. So, whenever you need to perform a call, your model calls the proxy instead and gets a response, which is formed in a way that is familiar to it. In case the third type of isolation is chosen, meaning that two bounded contexts are hosted in separate processes, the communication goes through the network. For a direct call, it is usually an HTTP call using REST or SOAP protocol. For an event, some sort of a message queue is used. In this situation, you don't have to create an anti-corruption layer between the two bounded contexts, because this messaging mechanism essentially acts as such.

Code Reuse Between Bounded Contexts

- Common code between Bounded Context1 & Bounded Context2
- DRY vs Proper boundaries

An important topic which often gets misunderstood is code reuse between bounded contexts. It might turn out that there is some code which is common for two bounded contexts, and which can be factored out and reused in both of them. The first temptation in such situation is to perform the extraction in order to comply with the don't repeat yourself principle. On the other hand, we have a guideline which says there should be strict boundaries between bounded contexts and developers should not allow concepts from one context to infiltrate to another. So, how to deal with this conflict?

- Business logic
  - Shouldn't be reused in most cases
  - Extract to a shared kernel
- Domain base classes
  - Reuse within a single team only
- Utility code
  - Reuse within a single team
  - Reuse across teams only if provides a lot of value

To answer this question, we need to define different types of code, which can be a potential subject for use. The first type is code that carries business logic. Such code should never be reused unless it has the exact same meaning for all bounded contexts involved. For example, you might have two bounded contexts, sales and support, which both contain a product entity. It may even be that these entities have some behavior in common. In this case, you still need to create separate entities for them in both bounded contexts and store them in distinct database tables. The reason here is that despite the fact these entities have some commonalities, they still represent different concepts. The sales perspective on what a product is is not the same as the support perspective on it, even if that is the same physical product. You shouldn't try to merge the two concepts into a single entity. At the same time, two domain classes might have the same meaning for different models. For example, both snack machine and ATM bounded contexts have identical perspective on the MoneyValueObject. It represents the same concept for both of them. If this is the case, you do need to reuse by it by extracting this class into a shared kernel like we did previously. It's a good idea to treat that kernel the same way you treat a bounded context, and strictly maintain its boundaries. The second type of code is domain base classes, such as entity value object repository, and so on. They don't contain any business logic themselves, but are still used by the actual domain classes in your bounded contexts. The answer to the question whether or not to use such code depends on the team configuration in your project. If you have the same team working on two bounded contexts, then it's a good idea to reuse domain base classes. On the contrary, if there are separate teams working on those models, they are better off to have their own implementations of those base classes, even if those implementations are identical. The reasoning behind this guideline is that despite the fact the base classes don't contain any business logic, they still are an additional point of coupling between the models. It is fine to have that point if you have a full control over the bounded contexts that use these base classes. Otherwise, it becomes a burden to maintain consistency in changes that are made by different teams. So, one set of base classes per each team, regardless of how many bounded contexts they are used in. In our application, we use the base classes, because we are the only team working on this project. The third type of code is utility code, code that doesn't contain any domain logic, but rather represents some useful helper methods. The guideline here is roughly the same as with the domain base classes. If a utility is small, such as Session Factory in our application, just duplicate it so that each team has its own set of helper methods. At the same time, if such code gets bigger and you see it can potentially provide a lot of failure to all teams in your company, create an internal open source project out of it. You can extract it to a separate project and make it publicly available to all teams in your company, but that should be something really useful, not just a set of random auxiliary classes. Overall, try to avoid reusing code between bounded contexts as much as possible, especially reusing the code from the domain layer. Extract a domain class to a shared kernel only when all bounded contexts involved have the same perspective on what it represents.

Implementing ATM Domain Logic

Alright, we are now ready to start implementing the second bounded context, the model of ATM. It will be simpler than the snack machine model. The only functionality it should contain is the ability to give the users cash in exchange for their bank cards balance. The ATM also needs to keep track of all charges made. This is how the implementation will look like. You can see it's a single entity with two fields, one for the MoneyInside and the other one for the MoneyCharged. We'll start off by working on the ATM entity. Note that for this project, I've chosen the first type of bounded context isolation, because the bounded context themselves are pretty small at this point. It means that we will gather all classes for the new bounded contexts in a separate folder. We won't create new projects for it. All right. Creating a new class, Atm.

```java
package ddd.logic.atm;
import static
ddd.logic.sharedKernel.Money.None;
import ddd.logic.common.AggregateRoot;
import ddd.logic.sharedKernel.Money;
public class Atm extends AggregateRoot {
    private static float commissionRate =
0.01f;
    private Money moneyInside = None;
    private float moneyCharged;
    public void takeMoney(float amount) {
        Money output =
moneyInside.allocate(amount);
        moneyInside =
moneyInside.substract(output);
        float amountWithCommission =
amount + amount * commissionRate;
        moneyCharged +=
amountWithCommission;
    }
    public void loadMoney(Money money) {
        moneyInside =
moneyInside.add(money);
    }
    public Money getMoneyInside() {
        return moneyInside;
    }
    protected void setMoneyInside(Money
moneyInside) {
        this.moneyInside = moneyInside;
```

```
    }
    public float getMoneyCharged() {
        return moneyCharged;
    }
    protected void setMoneyCharged(float
moneyCharged) {
        this.moneyCharged =
moneyCharged;
    }
}
```

This will be an aggregate root, so I inherit it from the AggregateRoot base class. The entity will contain two properties, MoneyInside and MoneyCharged, and I'm adding a method for taking money from the ATM. Now let's add some unit tests. Create an AtmTest.java. In src/test/java directory.

```
package ddd.logic;
import static org.junit.Assert.assertEquals;
import static
ddd.logic.sharedKernel.Money.Dollar;
import org.junit.Test;
import ddd.logic.atm.Atm;
public class AtmTest {
    @Test
    public void
take_money_exchanges_money_with_commiss
ion() {
        Atm atm = new Atm();
        atm.loadMoney(Dollar);
        atm.takeMoney(1);
        assertEquals(atm.getMoneyInside().
getAmount(), 0, 0);
        assertEquals(atm.getMoneyCharged
(), 1.01, 0.001);
    }
}
```

With the first test, we'll verify that the money inside the machine decreases and that it accounts the amount of money charged from a user. Creating an entity. In order to check the money inside the machine changes, we need to load it there first. So I'm calling a LoadMoney method here. Assuming there is a dollar inside the ATM, I as a user should be able to take it. After that, the amount of money inside must turn to 0, and the amount of money charged should be $1.01, because the commission for withdrawal is 1%. Creating the LoadMoney method, this method will just add whatever money will pass it to the MoneyInside property. We need to initialize the MoneyInside property with an empty instance. Okay, now the test fails for a good reason. It expects the MoneyInside to turn to 0, but sees there is still $1 inside. Let's implement the TakeMoney method. Just as with the snack machine model, here we allocate the required sum and extract it from the MoneyInside property. To calculate the charge amount, we need to compute the amount with commission and add it to the MoneyCharge property. Perfect. The test is passing.

There still are some requirements we need to take into account. For example, what if we try to take a single cent from the ATM? Should the commission be still charged in this case, and if so, how much should it be? Also, are there any rules for rounding the commission? For example, what if a user takes $1.10? Should the commission be one cent or two cents? These are the questions we should ask the domain expert. Let's say the expert replied that there should always be at least one cent commission for any withdrawal operation, and the commission itself should be rounded up to the next cent. Now as we have this knowledge, we can reflect it in our unit tests. With this test, we ensure that the commission is at least one cent.

```
@Test
    public void
commission_is_at_least_one_cent(){
        Atm atm = new Atm();
    atm.loadMoney(Cent);
    atm.takeMoney(0.01f);
    assertEquals(atm.getMoneyCharged(),
0.02, 0.001);
    }
```

You can see we load a cent into the Atm and take it back from it. The money charged should be two cents in this case. This test will make sure the commission is rounded properly.

```
@Test
    public void
commission_is_rounded_up_to_the_next_cent
(){
    Atm atm = new Atm();
    atm.loadMoney(Dollar.add(TenCent));
    atm.takeMoney(1.1f);
    assertEquals(atm.getMoneyCharged(),
1.12, 0.01);
    }
```

When we try to take $1.10, the machine should charge 2 cents as a commission, $1.12 overall. Both tests are failing currently. Let's implement the required functionality. So, in order to comply with these two requirements, we need a more sophisticated calculation algorithm for the chart sum. We cannot just multiply the amount by commission rate. Here is the function we will use for that purpose.

```
public float
caluculateAmountWithCommission(float
amount) {
```

```
        float commission = amount *
commissionRate;
        float lessThanCent = commission %
0.01f;
        if (lessThanCent > 0) {
            commission = commission -
lessThanCent + 0.01f;
        }
        return amount + commission;
    }
```

As you can see, it calculates the row commission amount first, and then determines if the amount contains a fraction which is less than a single cent. If there is such a fraction, the method replaces it with a cent, and returns the overall amount with the commission. We can replace this code here with a call to this method.

```
public void takeMoney(float amount) {
        Money output =
moneyInside.allocate(amount);
        moneyInside =
moneyInside.substract(output);
        float amountWithCommission =
caluculateAmountWithCommission(amount);
        moneyCharged +=
amountWithCommission;
}
```

The test has passed. The last thing we need to add is validations. We will use the same pattern we used previously. We will create a separate CanTake method, which will return an error string in case any of the preconditions are violated. So, what are they? First of all, we shouldn't be able to request 0 or a negative sum, it just doesn't make any sense in the context of ATM. Secondly, we need to check that the money inside the machine is sufficient to address the user's request. And finally, we need to check that the machine has enough change to pick the required sum. An empty string here would signalize no errors. After we enumerated all preconditions, we can use them in the TakeMoney method. And of course, it's a good idea to check these edge cases with unit tests. The Atm domain entity is ready.

```
public String canTakeMoney(float amount) {
        if (amount <= 0f)
                return "Invalid amount";
        if (moneyInside.getAmount() <
amount)
                return "Not enough money";
        if
(!moneyInside.canAllocate(amount))
                return "Not enough change";
        return "";
}

public void takeMoney(float amount) {
        if (canTakeMoney(amount) != "")
                throw new
IllegalStateException();

        Money output =
moneyInside.allocate(amount);
        moneyInside =
moneyInside.substract(output);
        float amountWithCommission =
caluculateAmountWithCommission(amount);
        moneyCharged +=
amountWithCommission;
}
```

Adjusting the database

Now as we have the domain class for the new bounded context ready, let's adjust our persistence layer. Here's the new AtmDto. We are ready to define the mapping between the entity and the database table. The mapping here is pretty simple.

```
package ddd.logic.atm;
import javax.persistence.Entity;
import javax.persistence.GeneratedValue;
import javax.persistence.Id;
import ddd.logic.sharedKernel.Money;
@Entity
public class AtmDto {
    @Id
    @GeneratedValue
    private long id;
    private float moneyCharged;
    private int oneCentCount;
    private int tenCentCount;
    private int quarterCount;
    private int oneDollarCount;
    private int fiveDollarCount;
    private int twentyDollarCount;
    @Transient
    private float amount ;
    public float getAmount() {
        return  amount;
    }
    @PostLoad
    public void setAmount() {
        amount = oneCentCount * 0.01f +
tenCentCount * 0.10f + quarterCount * 0.25f
+ oneDollarCount * 1f
```

```java
                    + fiveDollarCount * 5f +
twentyDollarCount * 20f;
    }
    // setters and getters for all the fields
    public Atm convertToAtm() {
        Atm atm = new Atm();
        atm.setId(id);
        atm.setMoneyCharged(moneyCharg
ed);
        atm.setMoneyInside(new
Money(oneCentCount,tenCentCount,quarter
Count,
                    oneDollarCount,fiveDollar
Count,twentyDollarCount));
        return atm;
    }
}
```

Spring boot will create the table for us. We
can see it in H2 console as shown in next page
by opening the link http://localhost:8080/h2-
console/login.do?jsessionid=05f13a4472a88758
3c538c3217fda1af in your web browser

Finally execute

```sql
insert into ATM_DTO (money_charged,
one_cent_count, one_dollar_count,
quarter_count, ten_cent_count,
five_dollar_count, twenty_dollar_count, id)
values (2.5,1, 1, 1, 1, 1, 1, 1);
```

In the H2 console.

- jdbc:h2:mem:testdb
- ☐ ATM_DTO
  - ⊞ ID
  - ⊞ FIVE_DOLLAR_COUNT
  - ⊞ MONEY_CHARGED
  - ⊞ ONE_CENT_COUNT
  - ⊞ ONE_DOLLAR_COUNT
  - ⊞ QUARTER_COUNT
  - ⊞ TEN_CENT_COUNT
  - ⊞ TWENTY_DOLLAR_COUNT
  - ⊞ Indexes
- ☐ HEAD_OFFICE_DTO
  - ⊞ ID
  - ⊞ BALANCE
  - ⊞ FIVE_DOLLAR_COUNT
  - ⊞ ONE_CENT_COUNT
  - ⊞ ONE_DOLLAR_COUNT
  - ⊞ QUARTER_COUNT
  - ⊞ TEN_CENT_COUNT
  - ⊞ TWENTY_DOLLAR_COUNT
  - ⊞ Indexes
- ☐ SLOT_DTO
  - ⊞ ID
  - ⊞ POSITION
  - ⊞ PRICE
  - ⊞ QUANTITY
  - ⊞ SNACK_DTO_ID
  - ⊞ SNACK_MACHINE_ID
  - ⊞ Indexes
- ☐ SNACK_DTO
  - ⊞ ID
  - ⊞ NAME
  - ⊞ Indexes
- ☐ SNACK_MACHINE_DTO
  - ⊞ ID
  - ⊞ FIVE_DOLLAR_COUNT
  - ⊞ MONEY_IN_TRANSACTION
  - ⊞ ONE_CENT_COUNT
  - ⊞ ONE_DOLLAR_COUNT
  - ⊞ QUARTER_COUNT
  - ⊞ TEN_CENT_COUNT
  - ⊞ TWENTY_DOLLAR_COUNT
  - ⊞ Indexes
- ⊞ INFORMATION_SCHEMA
- ⊞ Sequences
- ⊞ Users
- ⓘ H2 1.4.197 (2018-03-18)

The last thing is the repository.
package ddd.logic.atm;
import
org.springframework.data.repository.CrudRe
pository;
public interface AtmRepository extends
CrudRepository<AtmDto, Long> {
}
Spring boot will do rest of the magic. It will
provide the implementations to the repository.
We will not write any class to implement
AtmRepository interface.
We will use only methods to save , load etc.

Adding UI

At this point, we can define the user interface
for our model of Atm. I added a HTML view,
and AtmController for it.
This is how the UI looks like currently.

Money inside :$26.36
Money charged :$2.7

Take Money

No of coins and notes in Atm :
No. of 1 cent coin : 1   No. of 10 cent coin : 1   No. of 25 cent coin : 1
No. of 1 dollar note : 1   No. of 5 dollar note : 1   No. of 20 dollar note :

The idea is that we simulate the process of
withdrawal by inserting the required amount
in this text box and clicking on the Take
money button. You can see although the
values are displayed correctly, the interface

doesn't react on the button clicks. It will execute the takeMoney method, passing in the required amount dispensed. We will follow similar to SnackMachine Controller.

```java
package ddd.logic.atm;
import org.springframework.beans.factory.annotation.Autowired;
import org.springframework.stereotype.Controller;
import org.springframework.web.bind.annotation.GetMapping;
import org.springframework.web.bind.annotation.PathVariable;
import org.springframework.web.bind.annotation.PutMapping;
import org.springframework.web.bind.annotation.RequestMapping;
import org.springframework.web.bind.annotation.ResponseBody;
@Controller
@RequestMapping(path = "/atms")
public class AtmController {
    @Autowired
    private AtmRepository atmRepository;
    @Autowired
    private PaymentGateway paymentGateway;

    @GetMapping()
    @ResponseBody
    public List<AtmDto> getAtms() {
        List<AtmDto> list = new ArrayList<>();
```

```java
        atmRepository.findAll().forEach(list:
:add);
            return list;
    }
    @GetMapping("/{id}")
    @ResponseBody
    public AtmDto
getAtm(@PathVariable("id") long id) {
        return
atmRepository.findById(id).orElse(null);
    }

    @PutMapping("/{id}/{amount}")
    @ResponseBody
    public String
takeMoney(@PathVariable("id") long id,
@PathVariable("amount") float amount) {
        AtmDto atmDto =
atmRepository.findById(id).orElse(null);
        Atm atm = atmDto.convertToAtm();

        if(!atm.canTakeMoney(amount).isE
mpty()) return atm.canTakeMoney(amount);

        float amountWithCommission =
atm.caluculateAmountWithCommission(amou
nt);
        paymentGateway.chargePayment(a
mountWithCommission);
        atm.takeMoney(amount);

        atmRepository.save(atm.convertToA
tmDto());
        return "You have withrawn amount
: $"+ amount;
    }
}
public class Atm extends AggregateRoot {
```

```java
    public AtmDto convertToAtmDto() {
        AtmDto atmDto = new AtmDto();
        atmDto.setId(id);
        atmDto.setMoneyCharged(moneyCharged);        atmDto.setOneCentCount(moneyInside.getOneCentCount());        atmDto.setTenCentCount(moneyInside.getTenCentCount());        atmDto.setQuarterCount(moneyInside.getQuarterCount());        atmDto.setOneDollarCount(moneyInside.getOneDollarCount());        atmDto.setFiveDollarCount(moneyInside.getFiveDollarCount());
        atmDto.setTwentyDollarCount(moneyInside.getTwentyDollarCount());
        return atmDto;
    }
}
package ddd.logic.atm;
import org.springframework.data.repository.CrudRepository;
public interface AtmRepository extends CrudRepository<AtmDto, Long> {
}
package ddd.logic.atm;
import org.springframework.stereotype.Component;
@Component
public class PaymentGateway {
public void chargePayment(float amountWithCommission) {
    }
}
```

AtmView.html :
```html
<!DOCTYPE html>
<html>
<body>
 <span>Money inside :$<span id="moneyInside"></span></span>
```

```html
 </br>
 <span>Money charged :$<span
id="moneyCharged"></span></span>
 </br>
 </br>
 </br>
 <input type="text"
id="moneyToTake"><br>
 <button id="btnTakeMoney">Take Money
</button>
 </br>
 </br>
 </br>
 <div>No of coins and notes in Atm :</div>
 <table style="width:100%">
          </tr>
          <td>No. of 1 cent coin : <span
id="cent"></span></td>
          <td>No. of 10 cent coin : <span
id="tenCent"></span> </td>
          <td>No. of 25 cent coin : <span
id="quarter"></span> </td>
          </tr>
          </tr>
          <td>No. of 1 dollar note : <span
id="dollar"></span></td>
          <td>No. of 5 dollar note : <span
id="fiveDollar"></span></td>
          <td>No. of 20 dollar note : <span
id="twentyDollar"></span></td>
          </tr>
     </table>
<script src="../common/jquery-
3.3.1.js"></script>
<script src="atm.js"></script>
</body>
</html>
```

atm.js :

```javascript
let searchParams = new
URLSearchParams(window.location.search)
let param = '';
if(searchParams.has('id')){
    param = searchParams.get('id')
}else{
    param='1';
}
const rootURI =
"http://localhost:8080/atms/"+param;
getAtm();
function getAtm(){
    $.get(rootURI, function(data, status){
        $('#moneyInside').html(data.amount
);
        $('#moneyCharged').html(data.mone
yCharged);
        $('#cent').html(data.oneCentCount);
        $('#tenCent').html(data.tenCentCou
nt);
        $('#quarter').html(data.quarterCoun
t);
        $('#dollar').html(data.oneDollarCou
nt);
        $('#fiveDollar').html(data.fiveDollar
Count);
        $('#twentyDollar').html(data.twenty
DollarCount);
    });
}
$("#btnTakeMoney").click(function() {
    var moneyToTake =
$('#moneyToTake').val();
    $.ajax({
    url: rootURI+'/'+moneyToTake,
    type: 'PUT',
    success: function(data) {
      alert(data);
      location.reload();
```

```
      }
    });
});
```

Run LogicApplication.java as java application
to start our spring boot project. Execute the
insert sql (insert into ATM_DTO
(money_charged,one_cent_count,
one_dollar_count,
quarter_count, ten_cent_count,
five_dollar_count, twenty_dollar_count, id)
values (2.7,1, 1, 1, 1, 1, 1, 1);
) in H2 console to insert in Atm_dto table.
Let's try to withdraw the money now. I am
taking a dollar. As you can see, the number of
$1 notes inside the machine decreases, and the
money charged is set to $1.01. If I restart the
application, all parameters are still in place,
which means that the ATM was successfully
saved to the database. The last thing
remaining here is actual charging the value of
cash dispensed, plus 1% commission from the
user's bank card. We won't be writing the
actual code for this here, but I wanted to show
you the overall idea of how to do that. The
operation we are about to perform resides in
an external service, and the best way to work
with external services is create a proxy class
that wraps it with an API, which is
consumable for our Application Services.
Here's such a proxy class, PaymentGateway.
It's just a stop for a real gateway, but a real
world implementation would probably have
similar interface. It's important to understand
that in properly isolated model, domain
classes shouldn't work with such gateways.
The layer which is responsible for that is
Application Services, ViewModels in our case.
So, let's define a PaymentGateway here, and
instantiate it in the constructor. To use the

gateway, we need to know the amount to charge. In other words, we need to sum up the amount of money dispensed and the commission. We already have such methods in the ATM entity. All we need to do is make it public. And now we can calculate the amount, and charge the payment. And again, although the PaymentGateway doesn't do anything at this point, this code shows how you can approach this task. Alright, we have the ATM model implemented and working as requested.

Summary

- Bounded contexts
    - Provide boundaries for different models
    - Provide boundaries for ubiquitous language
- Bounded contexts vs sub-domains
    - 1-to-1 relation ideally (not always possible though)
- Context mapping
    - Reflects the current state of affairs, not a desired one
- Types of physical isolation
    - Start with the weakest isolation
    - Move forward only if necessary
- Communication between bounded contexts
- Code reuse
    - Avoid reusing domain classes
In this module, we discussed bounded contexts. Bounded contexts indicate boundaries between different models and

ubiquitous languages used in them. We talked about the relation between bounded contexts and sub-domains. The distinction between them is that sub-domains belong to the problem space, whereas bounded contexts is the solution for that problem. We discussed the 1-to-1 guideline. You should try to create a single bounded context for each sub-domain in your system. But keep in mind that it's not always possible. There are three reasons why you might want to depart from this practice. Legacy project, large code base, and large team. We talked about the importance of drawing a context map between bounded contexts. The main guideline here is that it should reflect the actual state of affairs, not the desired one. You learned three types of physical isolational bounded contexts. Keep in mind that while your code base is small, it makes sense not to separate bounded contexts physically and just keep them in a single jar. As the project grows, however, consider extracting different bounded contexts out of it to separate to your projects, or even to separate marker services. At the same time, make sure you maintain proper boundaries regardless of what type of physical isolation is chosen. We discussed communication between bounded contexts. It depends on the type of isolation you've chosen, and whether or not there is an anti-corruption layer between the contexts. We also talked about code reuse. The main rule here is that you should avoid reusing code that represents domain logic. In the next module, we will talk about domain events and two different ways of working with them.

Module 7: Working with Domain Events

Introduction

In this module, we will talk about domain events. We will see when they are applicable and how to actually represent them in code. We'll discuss way to work with domain events.

New Requirements

- Existing Functionality
  - Subdomain : Snack Machine
  - Subdomain : ATM
- New Functionality
  - Subdomain : Device Management
    - Tracking user payments
    - Moving cash

Now as we have two models, one for snack machine and the other for ATM, our stakeholders decided we need a new subsystem, which would be responsible for managing the devices. In the real world, a subsystem like this would probably do such tasks as setting new devices across the country, monitoring cash levels inside them, and so on. In our case, let's say it has only two requirements. Keeping track of all payments made by all users of our ATMs, and moving cash from snack machines to ATMs. So, whenever a user withdraws cash, the system should account the sum charged from the user's bank card and show us the total balance we have so far. The second requirement is about moving the cash the snack machines accumulated to ATMs. Such functionality makes sense, because snack machines produce cash so to speak, whereas ATMs consume it.

Introducing a New Bounded Context

- New sub-domain : Management
- New bounded context : Management
- Where the payments go?
- How cash flows from snack machines to ATMs?

Let's see how we can implement the new requirements in our domain model. From the previous module, we know that whenever we hear such words as subsystem, it's a strong sign there is a new sub-domain in the application, and there is. The new set of requirements this subsystem contains is completely different from the requirements we had previously. Let's call the new sub-domain Management. Following the 1-to-1 guideline we discussed in the previous module, we need to create a separate bounded context for it.

We need a new abstraction to help us keep track of all wireless payments and transfer cash from snack machines to ATMs. The best way to find a proper abstraction is to talk to the domain expert and ask the following questions. How the payments will be accounted? Where will they go? Also, how exactly the money will flow from snack machines to ATMs? Directly, or maybe there would be a transitional point? Let's say the domain expert replies that the money charged from the user's bank cards goes to our head office's bank account, and when we need to transfer cash from a snack machine to an ATM, we don't do it directly, but rather move it to the head office first and only after that send it to the ATM. Having this information in hand, we can start implementing the new functionality. This is how the new version of the context map looks like.

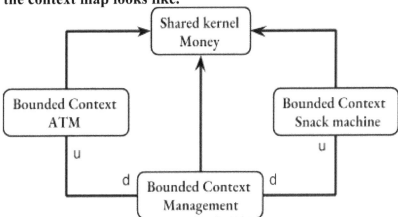

You can see it uses the short kernel with the Money value object, but it also relates to the other two bounded contexts. The relation between them is conformist, meaning that the Management bounded context conforms to whatever model the other two bounded contexts introduce. The letter u here means the bounded context is upstream, or master, in other words. The letter d means downstream or slave. The reason why the Management bounded context is conformist is because it will actively use the snack machine and ATM entities for transferring cash between them, so it makes sense to make it the new bounded context dependent on the existing two. With these answers, we can see there is a separate concept the domain expert used twice, the notion of head office. It is involved in both operations, so it is a good idea to introduce an entity with the same name to our domain model. Let's implement it. I am adding a new package (ddd.logic.management) for new bounded context, Management, and a new class HeadOffice. It would be a single entity aggregate. There would be two properties in it. The Balance property will keep track of all payments made from the user's bank cards, and the cash property will contain the cash transferred from the snack machines.

```
package ddd.logic.management;
import ddd.logic.common.AggregateRoot;
import ddd.logic.sharedKernel.Money;
public class HeadOffice extends
AggregateRoot {
    private float balance;
    private Money cash;
    public float getBalance() {
        return balance;
    }
    public void setBalance(float balance) {
        this.balance = balance;
    }
    public Money getCash() {
        return cash;
    }
    public void setCash(Money cash) {
```

```
        this.cash = cash;
    }
}
```

Let's now look at different ways of handling our new requirements.

Implementation

So far so good. We have a new bounded context defined. Let's see how we can implement the first requirement, how we can track all the charges made from the user's bank cards. The first option here is to place this logic to the Application Service AtmController.

```
public String
takeMoney(@PathParam("amount") float
amount) {
    // rest codes of this method are same as
shown previously
    HeadOffice headOffice =
getHeadOfficeInstance();

headOffice.setBalance(headOffice.getBalance(
) + amountWithCommission);
    officeRepository.save(headOffice);
}
```

So basically get an instance of the HeadOffice class somehow, for example, via its repository, increase the balance, and save the instance after that. Although it would work in our particular case to some extent, this approach has several drawbacks. First of all, such implementation means that we are coupling the AtmController to the HeadOffice entity. It means that we are introducing an additional

dependency between the ATM and
Management bounded contexts. With this
solution, not only Management knows about
ATMs, but ATM's bounded context also
becomes aware of Management. It's a good
idea to introduce as little coupling between
bounded contexts as possible and creating bi-
directional dependency here violates this
guideline. The second drawback is that this
approach works only until there is only a
single place where the takeMoney method is
called. If, for example, we add another
Controller to the ATM bounded context,
which would also dispense cash from an ATM
entity, we will need not to forget to repeat the
whole process with increasing the balance
again. So basically we will need to copy this
code to that new Controller. Obviously such
implementation would be error prone due to
code duplication and possible human factor.
The second option is to implement this
functionality in the takeMoney method of Atm
class itself.

```
public void takeMoney(float amount,
HeadOffice headOffice) {
     // rest are same
     headOffice.setBalance(headOffice.getBal
ance() + amountWithCommission);
     }
```

Add a new parameter, HeadOffice parameter,
and increase the balance by the amount with
commission. While this allows us to eliminate
the problem with code duplication, other
problems come into play. First, we still have
bi-directional coupling between the two
bounded contexts, which should be avoided
when possible. And second, and more
important, the ATM entity now gets a
responsibility which is not related to the ATM

itself. It is not the job of an ATM to increase the balance of the HeadOffice. Such duty just doesn't make sense in the context of our domain. It clearly violates the single responsibility principle. So how to solve this problem? The solution here is domain events. The ATM entity should raise an event about the charges that take place when the user withdraws cash, and the Management context should subscribe to those events and change the HeadOffice instance accordingly. This way we avoid introducing a bi-directional relationship between bounded contexts and stay away from the other problems we discussed here. We will see how to implement domain events later in this module. For now, let's take a closer look at this concept.

Domain Events

So, what is a domain event? A domain event represents an event that is significant for your domain model. It's important to distinguish usual events or system events from domain events. The former refer to such things as a button click, timer tick, window closed events, and so on. In other words, they represent notions that are related to the infrastructure. Domain events, on the other hand, describe occasions with are important for our domain. For example, when we click on the takeMoney button on the user interface, the click itself is a system event. Our domain doesn't care about it, just as it doesn't care about anything else on the user interface. At the same time, the domain operation, which happens after the

217

button click, namely the withdrawal operation, has a meaning for our domain. In our case, we need to account that operation and change the balance of the HeadOffice.

- Decouple Bounded Contexts
- Facilitate communication between Bounded Contexts
- Decouple entities within a single Bounded Context

Domain events are often used to decouple bounded contexts completely or replace bi-directional relationship with a uni-directional one. You saw an example of it in our application. Domain events will help us to avoid making the ATM bounded context aware of the Management bounded context. Along with direct calls, domain events is a technique for establishing communication between bounded contexts. Although it's the most common use case for domain events, it's not the only one. They can also be used for collaborating between entities within a single bounded context. It might be that an entity inside the bounded context should perform an action, which doesn't belong to the list of its responsibilities. In this case, it would be a good idea to introduce a domain event instead and perform that action elsewhere. You saw an example previously. The HeadOffice entity should react on every withdrawal in our domain model, and instead of adding the responsibility to change the balance to the ATM entity directly, we decided to create a domain event and thus free the ATM class from that duty.

Introducing a Domain Event

This is how the domain event will look, and this is where it will be used.
Domain event definition:

```
public class BalanceChangedEvent{
    public decimal delta;
    public BalanceChangedEvent(float delta) {
        this.delta = delta;
    }
}
```

Domain event generation:

```
public void takeMoney(float amount) {
        if (canTakeMoney(amount) != "")
            throw new
IllegalStateException();

        Money output =
moneyInside.allocate(amount);
        moneyInside =
moneyInside.substract(output);
        float amountWithCommission =
caluculateAmountWithCommission(amount);
        moneyCharged +=
amountWithCommission;
        // Raise the event
}
```

You can see instead of directly changing the balance of the HeadOffice here in the takeMoney method, we create an instance of the event and raise it. We will talk about the actual techniques for raising events later in this module. For now, let's discuss best practices for defining domain events themselves. The first guideline regards to the naming conventions.

- Naming : Past tense like BalanceChangedEvent
- Data : Include as little data as possible

As a domain event represents something that happened in the past, we should name them accordingly in the past tense. So, in our case, it is BalanceChangedEvent, not BalanceChange or ChangeBalance event. Also, try to be specific about what happened. Don't give generic names to your domain events. The next guideline here is that you should try to include as little data in the domain event as possible. Ideally it should contain only the information that is needed for the external code to react on this event, nothing more. In our case, you can see we include only the Delta, the sum that was charged from the user's bank card.

- Don't use domain classes to represent data in events
- Use primitive types instead

A question that often arises when it comes to defining an event is what data structure should one use to represent that information? Can we use entities and value objects for that?

```
class Person extends Entity{
    String firstName;
    String lastName;
}
class PersonChangedEvent{
    Person person;
    PersonChangedEvent(Person person){
        this.person= person;
    }
}
```

Above code :
- Include more information than needed
- Additional point of coupling

For example, if we had a person entity with this structure and we need to track changes in their first, last, and middle names, can we just create an event like this and include the person as a property in it? The answer is no. Doing so is generally a bad practice. The reason here is twofold. First of all, this way we almost always include more information to the domain event than needed, and that contradicts the first guideline. Secondly, with this implementation, we introduce an additional point of coupling between bounded contexts. It's basically fine if the bounded context consuming the event is connected to the bounded context which produces the event, and resides on the downstream side. In such a situation, the consuming bounded context has to conform to the producing bounded context anyway, meaning that it already knows about its internal structure, but it might not always be the case. It may be that two bounded contexts don't know of each other and still one of them is subscribed to the events from the other. In this case, adding a domain class, be it an entity or a value object to a domain event, adds a necessary coupling between the bounded contexts. So, the guideline here is to always represent data in domain events with primitive types only.
Id of the entity or full information about it?

- Ids : When consuming BC knows about producing BC
- Full information : When consuming BC doesn't know about producing B

Another frequent question is whether to include an ID of the changed entity or enclose full information about it in the domain event? The answer to this question depends on the relationship between producing and consuming bounded contexts. If the bounded contexts that are subscribed to the event already collaborate with the context which originates the event, it's fine to use Ids. The downstream bounded contexts will be able to query information about the entity on receiving the event. We don't introduce any additional coupling here. At the same time, if they don't know about the bounded contexts producing the event, we have to enclose full data with regard to the changed fields of the entity to the event. But again, we must use primitive types to represent this data and not use the entity itself.

Physical Delivery

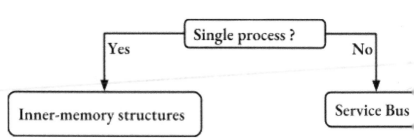

- Physical delivery is orthogonal to the notion of domain events

When working with domain events, another question that inevitably arises is how to deliver them physically to the subscribers? The answer depends on what type of physical isolation is used for bounded contexts. If the bounded contexts reside in a single process, then the delivery isn't actually a matter because the code in those bounded contexts share the computer memory. In the case of separate processes, the delivery goes via the network using some sort of a service bus. We will look at some of the techniques later in this module, but we will not dive deep into them in this book. However, I want to emphasize that just as physical isolation of bounded contexts is orthogonal to the logical isolation, physical delivery of domain events is not related to the logical counterpart. We can use whatever delivery technique we want. We can even persist the events and use them later in an event-sourcing architecture. All such techniques use the same logical concept of a domain event behind the scene.

Building up Management Bounded Context

Before we move forward with domain events, let's build up the Management bounded context and introduce persistence for it..

```
package ddd.logic.management;
import javax.persistence.Entity;
import javax.persistence.GeneratedValue;
import javax.persistence.Id;
import javax.persistence.PostLoad;
import javax.persistence.Transient;
import ddd.logic.sharedKernel.Money;
@Entity
public class HeadOfficeDto {
    @Id
    @GeneratedValue
    private long id;
    private float balance;
    private int oneCentCount;
    private int tenCentCount;
    private int quarterCount;
    private int oneDollarCount;
```

```java
    private int fiveDollarCount;
    private int twentyDollarCount;

    @Transient
    private float amount ;
    public float getAmount() {
        return  amount;
    }
    @PostLoad
    public void setAmount() {
        amount = oneCentCount * 0.01f +
tenCentCount * 0.10f + quarterCount * 0.25f
+ oneDollarCount * 1f
                    + fiveDollarCount * 5f +
twentyDollarCount * 20f;
    }

    public HeadOffice
convertToHeadOffice() {
        HeadOffice headOffice = new
HeadOffice();
        headOffice.setId(id);
        headOffice.setBalance(balance);
        headOffice.setCash(new
Money(oneCentCount,tenCentCount,quarter
Count,
                    oneDollarCount,fiveDollar
Count,twentyDollarCount));
        return headOffice;
    }
// generate setters and getters for all fields
}
```

Now restart the Application by running
LogicApplication.java as a java application.
Spring boot will automatically create table for
us . Lets see that table in H2 console. Open
http://localhost:8080/h2-
console/login.do?jsessionid=110059b79b165f4
987214bc9305eb2a4 in browser

- HEAD_OFFICE_DTO
  - ID
    - BIGINT(19) NOT NULL
  - BALANCE
    - DOUBLE(17) NOT NULL
  - FIVE_DOLLAR_COUNT
    - INTEGER(10) NOT NULL
  - ONE_CENT_COUNT
    - INTEGER(10) NOT NULL
  - ONE_DOLLAR_COUNT
    - INTEGER(10) NOT NULL
  - QUARTER_COUNT
    - INTEGER(10) NOT NULL
  - TEN_CENT_COUNT
    - INTEGER(10) NOT NULL
  - TWENTY_DOLLAR_COUNT
    - INTEGER(10) NOT NULL
  - Indexes
    - PRIMARY_KEY_E

Once again, note that we are inlining the Money value object here. Along with Money, the table also contains the balance column. The HeadOffice entity will need a functionality to change the balance, so we can add a changeBalance method to it, and initialize the cash property.

```
public class HeadOffice extends
AggregateRoot {
   private Money cash = None;
   public void changeBalance(float delta){
      balance += delta;
   }
   public HeadOfficeDto
convertToHeadOfficeDto() {
        HeadOfficeDto headOfficeDto = new
HeadOfficeDto();
        headOfficeDto.setId(id);
        headOfficeDto.setBalance(balance);
```

```java
headOfficeDto.setOneCentCount(cash.getOne
CentCount());
headOfficeDto.setTenCentCount(cash.getTen
CentCount());
headOfficeDto.setQuarterCount(cash.getQuar
terCount());
headOfficeDto.setOneDollarCount(cash.getOn
eDollarCount());
headOfficeDto.setFiveDollarCount(cash.getFi
veDollarCount());
headOfficeDto.setTwentyDollarCount(cash.ge
tTwentyDollarCount());
        return headOfficeDto;
    }
//rest codes are same
}
```

Next we need to add a repository for that aggregate, HeadOfficeRepository.

```java
package ddd.logic.management;
import
org.springframework.data.repository.CrudRe
pository;
public interface HeadOfficeRepository
extends CrudRepository<HeadOfficeDto,
Long> {}
```

Spring Boot will do the remaining magic. And lastly, we need to think about how we will access the HeadOffice. Our stakeholders currently have only one HeadOffice, so it's a good idea to reflect it in our domain model. It doesn't make a lot of sense to always retrieve that single instance from the database. What we can do instead is we can employ the singleton design pattern and keep a reference to the HeadOffice instance during the entire application lifetime. We can implement the singleton pattern by adding a new class, HeadOfficeInstance. This class will hold the reference and our code will access it when needed instead of fetching it from the repository. We know that the only HeadOffice in our domain model has the ID of one, so we can specify it here as a constant. And finally, we need to initialize the singleton by fetching the proper object from the database.

```
package ddd.logic.management;
import
org.springframework.beans.factory.annotatio
n.Autowired;
import
org.springframework.stereotype.Component;
@Component
public class HeadOfficeInstance {
    @Autowired
    private HeadOfficeRepository
headOfficeRepository;
    private static long HeadOfficeId = 1;
    private HeadOfficeDto headOfficeDto;
    public HeadOfficeDto getInstance() {
        return
headOfficeRepository.findById(HeadOfficeId)
.orElse(null);
    }
}
```

You might wonder where in the onion architecture this class resides. It plays the same role as a repository, so it resides in the second innermost layer on this diagram. It means that classes from inner most layer cannot access it. Only classes from the same layer or upper can work with this singleton. We didn't implement this functionality in the HeadOfficeRepository itself, because it would violate the single responsibility principle. Repositories should fetch objects from the database and save it back. They shouldn't hold instances of anything. That's a task for another domain class.

The HeadOffice entity is ready, and now we need to bind these two classes(Atm and HeadOfiice). So basically when a user takes money, we need to change the balance of our HeadOffice by passing in the amount of money the ATM charged from the user. That's where domain events will help us.

Handling Domain Events with Spring Boot

Spring allows to create and publish custom events which – by default – are synchronous
- the event should extend ApplicationEvent
- the listener should implement the ApplicationListener interface
- the publisher should inject an ApplicationEventPublisher object

All right, now we are ready to create a class for the event we discussed previously, BalanceChangedEvent.

```
package ddd.logic.atm;
import
org.springframework.context.ApplicationEve
nt;
public class BalanceChangedEvent extends
ApplicationEvent {
    public float delta;
    public BalanceChangedEvent(Object
source, float delta) {
        super(source);
        this.delta = delta;
    }
    public float getDelta() {
```

```
        return delta;
    }
}
```

Now we are ready to create a class for the event handler.

```
package ddd.logic.management;
import
org.springframework.beans.factory.annotatio
n.Autowired;
import
org.springframework.context.ApplicationListe
ner;
import
org.springframework.stereotype.Component;
import ddd.logic.atm.BalanceChangedEvent;
@Component
public class BalanceChangedEventHandler
implements
ApplicationListener<BalanceChangedEvent>
{
    @Autowired
    private HeadOfficeInstance
headOfficeInstance;
    @Autowired
    private HeadOfficeRepository
headOfficeRepository;
    @Override
    public void
onApplicationEvent(BalanceChangedEvent
domainEvent) {
        HeadOfficeDto headOfficeDto =
headOfficeInstance.getInstance();
        HeadOffice headOffice =
headOfficeDto.convertToHeadOffice();
        headOffice.changeBalance(domainE
vent.getDelta());
        headOfficeRepository.save(headOffi
ce.convertToHeadOfficeDto());
    }
```

}
To implement it, we need to create a repository, get the HeadOfficeInstance, change the balance using the data passed with the event, and save the Office. This will be the handler implementation. Handlers are usually quite simple, because what they often do is just delegate the actual work to other domain classes. You can think of event handlers as of domain services. Their roles are very similar. We'll talk about domain services in more detail in the next module. Note that the event itself is defined in the ATM bounded context, whereas the handler for it in the Management context. It is no coincidence, because it reflects the actual relation between the bounded contexts. The ATM bounded context generates the event and the management bounded context consumes it and reacts accordingly. It also allows us to preserve the uni-directional relationship between them. So how can we glue the event and the event handler together? All right, to actually raise the events, we need to modify AtmController.

```
public class AtmController {
    @Autowired
    private ApplicationEventPublisher applicationEventPublisher;     public String takeMoney(@PathVariable("id") long id, @PathVariable("amount") float amount) {
//rest codes of this method are same as previous

        atmDto = atm.convertToAtmDto();
        atmRepository.save(atmDto);
        dispatchEvents(atmDto);
        return "You have withrawn amount : $"+ amount;
    }
```

```java
    private void dispatchEvents(AtmDto
atmDto) {
        if (atmDto == null) return;
        for (ApplicationEvent domainEvent :
atmDto.getDomainEvents()) {
            applicationEventPublisher.publi
shEvent(domainEvent);
        }
        atmDto.clearEvents();
    }
//rest codes of this class are same as previous
}
```

Now atmDto.getDomainEvents() will return null because atmDto do not have domain events.Lets fix it. Modify AggregateRoot.java , Atm,java and AtmDto.java

```java
package ddd.logic.common;
import java.util.ArrayList;
import java.util.List;
import
org.springframework.context.ApplicationEve
nt;
public abstract class AggregateRoot extends
Entity {
    private List<ApplicationEvent>
domainEvents = new
ArrayList<ApplicationEvent>();
    protected void
addDomainEvent(ApplicationEvent
newEvent) {
        domainEvents.add(newEvent);
    }
    public void clearEvents() {
        domainEvents.clear();
    }
    public List<ApplicationEvent>
getDomainEvents() {
        return domainEvents;
```

```java
        }
}
public class Atm extends AggregateRoot {
    public AtmDto convertToAtmDto() {
        //rest code of this method are same as
previous
        atmDto.setDomainEvents(getDomain
Events());
        return atmDto;
    }
}
public class AtmDto {
    @Transient
    @JsonIgnore
    private List<ApplicationEvent>
domainEvents;
    public void clearEvents() {
        domainEvents.clear();
    }
    public List<ApplicationEvent>
getDomainEvents() {
        return domainEvents;
    }
    public void
setDomainEvents(List<ApplicationEvent>
domainEvents) {
        this.domainEvents = domainEvents;
    }
// rest codes are same
}
```

Note that such implementation fits into the notion of unit of work.

This is best expressed with an example.

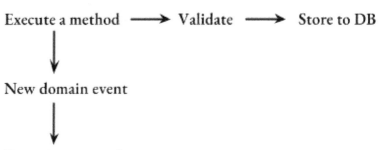

Execute a method ⟶ Validate ⟶ Store to DB

New domain event

Event is processed

Let's say that we start a business operation. It first executes a method which results in a domain event, employs some validations next, and finally saves everything into the database. The happy path in this case works fine, an event is produced, the subscriber successfully consumed, all validations pass, and all data is persisted. But we'll get a problem in case the validation fails, and we need to terminate the operation. The problem is that the domain event is already raised and processed by the time the validation fails, and there is no easy way for us to rollback the changes made. This is why in AtmController we save and then after successful save we process the event. atmRepository.save(atmDto); dispatchEvents(atmDto); This implementation fits the notion of unit of work. Another advantage of this. We could change the balance of an ATM for several times during the single business transaction, and each time we do that, a new event is raised and stored in list and then process at once. Our domain entity is no longer responsible for raising it. All it does it saves it to the internal list. All right, we have entities with domain events attached to them. How can we process those events, and not only just process, but do that in a way that allows us to preserve the

233

unit of work semantics? In other words, take an action only when the business transaction is committed.

Recap

Let's recap what we've done in the previous demo. First of all, we split the two responsibilities that were bound together before that, creating a domain event and dispatching it. Our entities are now responsible for the creation of events only. The actual dispatching is given away to the infrastructure. This implementation allows us to preserve the isolation for our domain model and also adhere to the notion of unit of work. In terms of processing the events, we rely on the internal Spring Boot mechanics, which gives us a great opportunity to extend its behavior with our own code. We dispatch the domain events only after the persistence is completed. This allows us to maintain consistency between the changes made to our aggregates and the domain events we raise. Also, note that we defined the collection of domain events in the AggregateRoot base class. That's no coincidence. Just as aggregate roots are responsible for maintaining aggregate invariants and consistency boundaries, they are also responsible for all domain events occurred in the aggregate.

Using Domain Events to Communicate Between Microservices

As you can see now, domain events is a powerful tool which facilitates communication between bounded contexts. I mentioned earlier that you can use the concept of domain events regardless of what type of physical delivery is chosen for them. Here I want to show you an example of how you can implement communication between bounded contexts, which reside in separate processes. In other words, between microservices.

```
public class BalanceChangedEventHandler implements
IHandler<BalanceChangedEvent> {
    public void
handle(BalanceChangedEvent domainEvent) {
        EsbGateway.getInstance().sendBalanceChangedMessage(domainEvent.getDelta())
    }
}
```

This is how we could send domain events to other microservices. You can see this is the same event handler as before, but this time instead of executing the actual code for handling the event, it sends an ESB message via a message bus. This message is then received and processed by whatever microservice is listening to these particular kind of events coming from the message bus. Also note that this version of the handler resides in the ATM bounded context. That's because the responsibility to send the event to the message bus lies on the bounded context producing it.

Adding Interface for the Management Bounded Context

Alright, we are done with the first requirement, keeping track of all charges made from the user's bank cards. The second requirement we have is moving cash from snack machines to ATMs. We won't dive deep into it too much here, because the solution is pretty straightforward, but I wanted to show you the end result and point out some key elements of the implementation. This is our head office dashboard.

Balance : $20.2
Cash : $2636

Snack machines	ATMs
Id Money 1 $0 2 $263.6	Id Cash 1 $1298 2 $527.2

Move cash from Snack machine to Head office :

| Enter SnackMachine Id | Unload |

Move cash from Head office to Atm :

| Enter Atm Id | Load |

And here is the html code :
HeadOfficeView.html
```
<html>
<body>
    <div>
        Balance : $<span
id="balance"></span>
    </div>
    <div>
        Cash : $<span id="cash"></span>
    </div>
    </br>
    <table style="width: 100%"
border="1">
        <tr>
            <th>Snack machines</th>
            <th>ATMs</th>
        </tr>
```

```html
<tr>
    <td>
        <table style="width: 100%">
            <tr>
                <td>
                    <ul id="snackMachineList" type="none">
                        <li><span>Id</span>  <span>Money</span></li>
                    </ul>
                </td>
            </tr>
        </table>
    </td>
    <td>
        <table style="width: 100%">
            <tr>
                <td>
                    <ul id="atmList" type="none">
                        <li><span>Id</span>  <span>Cash</span></li>
                    </ul>
                </td>
            </tr>
            <!-- <tr>
                <td>Id</td>
                <td>Cash</td>
            </tr>
            <tr>
                <td id="atmId">1</td>
                <td id="cash">$4</td>
```

```html
                                         <td><a
href="../atm/AtmView.html">Show</a></td>
                                            <td><button
id="btnLoad">
                                                        Load
cash
                                                      </buton>
</td>
                                       </tr> -->
                               </table>
                           </td>
                    </tr>
             </table>
             </br>
             </br>
             </br>
             <div>Move cash from Snack machine to
Head office :</div>
             <input type="text"
id="snackmachineId" placeholder="Enter
SnackMachine Id"></>
         <button id="btnUnload">Unload</button>
         </br>
             </br>
             </br>
             <div>Move cash from Head office to Atm
:</div>
             <input type="text" id="atmId"
placeholder="Enter Atm Id"></>
         <button id="btnLoad">Load</button>
             <script src="../common/jquery-
3.3.1.js"></script>
             <script src="headOffice.js"></script>
</body>
</html>
```

It displays a list of all snack machines in our
system, as well as a list of all ATMs. You can
see it also shows the balance of the head office
itself and the amount of total cash it stores.

239

I will show you the actual workflow of transmitting cash from a snack machine to an ATM. To use a snack machine, we can display it by clicking on id link of the snack machine . Suppose initially all money are 0 . Here let's say, for example, that I want to buy a chocolate. I've inserted $3 and buying it. After I come back to head office window, you can see the amount of money in snack machine in the list changes to $3. I can now unload the money from the snack machine to the head office by entering the snack machine id in the text field and then clicking on unload button. Now money in snack machine becomes 0 and cash of head office changes to $3. We can also load this head office $3 money to the ATM by entering the atm id in text field and clicking on load button.Now money inside head office becomes 0 and money inside atm becomes $3. Now i click on atm id to open Atm window. Now I as a user of the ATM I take $3 from the ATM. Now come to head office window. You can see the balance of our head office has changed to $0.03,.meaning that our head office just earned 3 cents. And money inside Atm becomes 0. To implement the actual functionality, I added two methods to the head office class.

```
public class HeadOffice extends
AggregateRoot
    public void
unloadCashFromSnackMachine(SnackMachi
ne snackMachine){
    Money money =
snackMachine.unloadMoney();
    cash = cash.add(money);
  }
  public void loadCashToAtm(Atm atm){
    atm.loadMoney(cash);
```

```java
        cash = Money.None;
    }
//rest are same
}
public class SnackMachine extends
AggregateRoot {
    public Money unloadMoney() {
        if (moneyInTransaction > 0)
            throw new
IllegalStateException();
        Money money = moneyInside;
        moneyInside = Money.None;
        return money;
    }
//rest are same
}
```

One for unloading cash from a snack machine and another one for loading it to an ATM. And here the HeadOfficeController

```java
package ddd.logic.management;
import
org.springframework.beans.factory.annotatio
n.Autowired;
import
org.springframework.stereotype.Controller;
import
org.springframework.web.bind.annotation.Ge
tMapping;
import
org.springframework.web.bind.annotation.Pat
hVariable;
import
org.springframework.web.bind.annotation.Pu
tMapping;
import
org.springframework.web.bind.annotation.Re
questMapping;
```

```java
import
org.springframework.web.bind.annotation.Re
sponseBody;
import ddd.logic.atm.Atm;
import ddd.logic.atm.AtmDto;
import ddd.logic.atm.AtmRepository;
import ddd.logic.management.HeadOffice;
import ddd.logic.management.HeadOfficeDto;
import
ddd.logic.management.HeadOfficeInstance;
import
ddd.logic.management.HeadOfficeRepository;
import
ddd.logic.snackMachine.SnackMachine;
import
ddd.logic.snackMachine.SnackMachineDto;
import
ddd.logic.snackMachine.SnackMachineReposi
tory;
@Controller
@RequestMapping(path = "/headOffice")
public class HeadOfficeController {
    @Autowired
    private SnackMachineRepository
snackMachineRepository;
    @Autowired
    private AtmRepository atmRepository;
    @Autowired
    private HeadOfficeRepository
headOfficeRepository;
    @Autowired
    private HeadOfficeInstance
headOfficeInstance;

    @GetMapping
    @ResponseBody
    public HeadOfficeDto getHeadOffice() {
        return
headOfficeInstance.getInstance();
```

```java
    }
    @PutMapping("/{atmId}/loadCash")
    public void
loadCashToAtm(@PathVariable("atmId")
long atmId) {
        AtmDto atmDto =
atmRepository.findById(atmId).orElse(null);
        HeadOfficeDto headOfficeDto =
headOfficeInstance.getInstance();
        Atm atm = atmDto.convertToAtm();
        HeadOffice headOffice =
headOfficeDto.convertToHeadOffice();
        headOffice.loadCashToAtm(atm);
        atmRepository.save(atm.convertToA
tmDto());
        headOfficeRepository.save(headOffi
ce.convertToHeadOfficeDto());
    }
    @PutMapping("/{snackMachineId}/unlo
adCash")
    public void
unloadCash(@PathVariable("snackMachineI
d") long snackMachineId) {
        SnackMachineDto snackMachineDto
=
snackMachineRepository.findById(snackMac
hineId).orElse(null);
        if (snackMachineDto == null) return;
        HeadOfficeDto headOfficeDto =
headOfficeInstance.getInstance();
        HeadOffice headOffice =
headOfficeDto.convertToHeadOffice();
        SnackMachine snackMachine =
snackMachineDto.convertToSnackMachine();
        headOffice.unloadCashFromSnack
Machine(snackMachine);
        snackMachineRepository.save(snack
Machine.convertToSnackMachineDto());
```

```
        headOfficeRepository.save(headOffi
ce.convertToHeadOfficeDto());
    }
}
```

And now we will see the the java script file headOffice.js in next page to connect HTML file HeadOfficeView to the HeadOfficeController.java.

headOffice.js :

```
const headOfficeUri =
"http://localhost:8080/headOffice";
getHeadOffice();
function getHeadOffice(){
    $.get(headOfficeUri, function(data,
status){
        $('#cash').html(data.amount);
        $('#balance').html(data.balance);
    });
}
const snackMachineUri =
"http://localhost:8080/snackmachines";
getSnackMachines();
function getSnackMachines(){
    $.get(snackMachineUri, function(data,
status){
        var list = data == null ? [] : (data
instanceof Array ? data : [data]);

        $.each(list, function(index, item) {
            $('#snackMachineList').append(
            '<li><a
href="../snackMachine/SnackMachineView.ht
ml?id='+item.id+'">'+item.id+'</a> &n
bsp  <span>$'+item.amount+'</sp
an></li>');
        });
    });
}
const atmUri = "http://localhost:8080/atms";
```

```javascript
getAtms();
function getAtms(){
    $.get(atmUri, function(data, status){
        var list = data == null ? [] : (data
instanceof Array ? data : [data]);

        $.each(list, function(index, item) {
            $('#atmList').append(
            '<li><a
href="../atm/AtmView.html?id='+item.id+'">'
+item.id+'</a>    <spa
n>$'+item.amount+'</span></li>');
        });
    });
}
$("#btnUnload").click(function() {
    var snackmachineId =
$('#snackmachineId').val();
    $.ajax({
    url:
headOfficeUri+'/'+snackmachineId+'/unloadC
ash',
    type: 'PUT',
    success: function(data) {
    }
    });
});
$("#btnLoad").click(function() {
    var atmId = $('#atmId').val();
    $.ajax({
    url:
headOfficeUri+'/'+atmId+'/loadCash',
    type: 'PUT',
    success: function(data) {
    }
    });
});
```

In the next page you can see the overall structure of our final Spring Boot project named "logic" in Eclipse IDE.

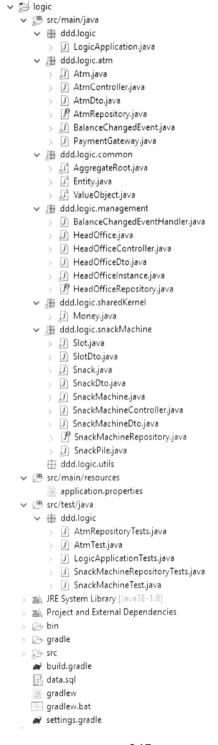

- logic
  - src/main/java
    - ddd.logic
      - LogicApplication.java
    - ddd.logic.atm
      - Atm.java
      - AtmController.java
      - AtmDto.java
      - AtmRepository.java
      - BalanceChangedEvent.java
      - PaymentGateway.java
    - ddd.logic.common
      - AggregateRoot.java
      - Entity.java
      - ValueObject.java
    - ddd.logic.management
      - BalanceChangedEventHandler.java
      - HeadOffice.java
      - HeadOfficeController.java
      - HeadOfficeDto.java
      - HeadOfficeInstance.java
      - HeadOfficeRepository.java
    - ddd.logic.sharedKernel
      - Money.java
    - ddd.logic.snackMachine
      - Slot.java
      - SlotDto.java
      - Snack.java
      - SnackDto.java
      - SnackMachine.java
      - SnackMachineController.java
      - SnackMachineDto.java
      - SnackMachineRepository.java
      - SnackPile.java
    - ddd.logic.utils
  - src/main/resources
    - application.properties
  - src/test/java
    - ddd.logic
      - AtmRepositoryTests.java
      - AtmTest.java
      - LogicApplicationTests.java
      - SnackMachineRepositoryTests.java
      - SnackMachineTest.java
  - JRE System Library [JavaSE-1.8]
  - Project and External Dependencies
  - bin
  - gradle
  - src
  - build.gradle
  - data.sql
  - gradlew
  - gradlew.bat
  - settings.gradle

Ande here is our the final static web project for user interface, project name is UI :

- ∨ 🖳 UI
  - 〉 ≣\ JavaScript Resources
  - ∨ 🗁 WebContent
    - ∨ 🗁 atm
      - 〉 📄 atm.js
      - 📄 AtmView.html
    - ∨ 🗁 common
      - 〉 📄 jquery-3.3.1.js
    - ∨ 🗁 headOffice
      - 〉 📄 headOffice.js
      - 📄 HeadOfficeView.html
    - ∨ 🗁 snackMachine
      - 〉 📄 snackMachine.js
      - 📄 SnackMachineView.html

To test the final Application . Fist run the logic spring boot project as a java application. Execute the below data.sql(shown in next page) file content in H2 database console and open the static web UI project in browser. Data.sql:
insert into snack_dto (name, id) values ('Chocolate', 1);
insert into snack_dto (name, id) values ('Soda', 2);
insert into snack_dto (name, id) values ('Gum', 3);
insert into snack_machine_dto (five_dollar_count, money_in_transaction, one_cent_count, one_dollar_count, quarter_count, ten_cent_count, twenty_dollar_count, id) values (100, 0.0, 100, 100, 100, 100, 100, 1);
insert into slot_dto (position, price, quantity, snack_dto_id, id) values (1, 40.0, 100, 1, 2);
insert into slot_dto (position, price, quantity, snack_dto_id, id) values (2, 20.0, 100, 2, 3);

insert into slot_dto (position, price, quantity, snack_dto_id, id) values (3, 10.0, 100, 3, 4);
update slot_dto set snack_machine_id=1 where id=2;
update slot_dto set snack_machine_id=1 where id=3;
update slot_dto set snack_machine_id=1 where id=4;
insert into snack_machine_dto (five_dollar_count, money_in_transaction, one_cent_count, one_dollar_count, quarter_count, ten_cent_count, twenty_dollar_count, id) values (10, 0.0, 10, 10, 10, 10, 10, 2);
insert into slot_dto (position, price, quantity, snack_dto_id, id) values (1, 40.0, 100, 1, 5);
insert into slot_dto (position, price, quantity, snack_dto_id, id) values (2, 20.0, 100, 2, 6);
insert into slot_dto (position, price, quantity, snack_dto_id, id) values (3, 10.0, 100, 3, 7);
update slot_dto set snack_machine_id=2 where id=5;
update slot_dto set snack_machine_id=2 where id=6;
update slot_dto set snack_machine_id=2 where id=7;
insert into ATM_DTO (money_charged,one_cent_count, one_dollar_count, quarter_count, ten_cent_count, five_dollar_count, twenty_dollar_count, id) values (0,50, 50, 50, 50, 50, 50, 1);
insert into ATM_DTO (money_charged,one_cent_count, one_dollar_count, quarter_count, ten_cent_count, five_dollar_count, twenty_dollar_count, id) values (0,20, 20, 20, 20, 20, 20, 2);

```
insert into HEAD_OFFICE_DTO
(balance,one_cent_count, one_dollar_count,
quarter_count, ten_cent_count,
five_dollar_count, twenty_dollar_count,  id)
values (0,0, 0, 0, 0, 0, 0, 1);
```

Summary

- **Domain Events**
- **Best practices for defining a Domain Event**
    - **Naming in the past tense**
    - **Include as little data as possible**
    - **Don't include domain classes**
    - **Id vs full information**
- **Physical delivery of Domain Events is an orthogonal topic**
- **Way of handling domain events**
- **Don't use domain entities to display data on the screen**

In this module, we talked about domain events. Domain events is a great tool that helps us keep bounded contexts decoupled from each other. You saw how awkward code might be without them. Although communication between bounded contexts is the most common use case for domain events, they can also be employed for decoupling classes inside a single bounded context. We discussed four best practices for defining domain events. First, keep the name in the past tense. Second, try to include as little data in a domain event as possible. Ideally it should contain only the information that is needed for the external code to react on this event, nothing more. Third, don't include domain classes such as entities and value objects into domain events. It would introduce a necessary coupling between bounded contexts. And finally, include full information about changed objects in the case consuming bounded contexts don't know about the bounded contexts producing the event. In case they know about it, you can include just an ID of the changed entity. We touched upon physical delivery of domain events. The main point here is that how exactly domain events are delivered to consuming bounded contexts is orthogonal to the notion of domain event itself. The techniques for working with them in the domain model remain the same. You saw way of handling domain events. That way we keep our domain model isolated and also adhere to the notion of unit of work.

Module 8: Looking Forward to Further Enhancements

Introduction

In this module, we will discuss DDD concepts that we didn't cover in our sample project, and some further possible ways in which our application can evolve in the future. We will also look at some common anti-patterns programmers employ when they start applying DDD principles in practice.

Always Valid vs. Not Always Valid

One of the debatable topics in DDD is whether to always keep entities and value objects in a valid state or allow them to reside in an invalid state and check that state later on; for example, before saving them to the database. This topic is best expressed with an example. Let's say we have a domain entity cargo with a Max Weight property. Let's also say it contains several items, each of which has its own weight, and there is an invariant saying that the cargo cannot contain a number of items the total of weight which exceeds the maximum weight the cargo can handle. This is how we could express the domain adherent to the Always Valid approach.

```
public class Cargo extends AggregateRoot{
private int maxWeight;
private List<Product> items;
public Cargo(int maxWeight){
this.maxWeight= maxWeight;
items= newList<Product>();
}
public void addItem(Product product){
int currentWeight =
items.stream().mapToInt(x -> x.weight).sum();
if(currentWeight+ product.weight >
maxWeight)
```

```
throw new InvalidStateException();
items.add(product);
}
}
```

You can see we first create a cargo with some maxWeight value, and then check that this maximum weight would not be exceeded in the addItem method call. If it is, we throw an exception signalizing that the invariant of the entity is violated. That way we don't allow the class to enter an invalid state. This is, on the other hand, how we could solve the problem adherent to the Not Always Valid approach.

```
public class Cargo extends AggregateRoot{
public int maxWeight;
private List<Product> Items;
public Cargo(int maxWeight){
maxWeight = maxWeight;
items= newList<Product>();
}
public void addItem(Product product){
items.add(product);
}
public boolean isValid(){
int currentWeight =
items.stream().mapToInt(x -> x.weight).sum();
return currentWeight<= MaxWeight;
}
}
```

You can see we allow any number of products to be added to the cargo. To validate whether or not the invariants are broken, we introduce a separate isValid method. Both techniques have their own pros and cons.

- Always valid : Don't have to worry about validation
- Not always valid : Gather most validations in one place

The main benefit of the always valid approach is that we as programmers can be sure that objects we are working with always reside in a valid state whenever we accept them as int parameters, or get them as a result of some operation. On the other hand, the Not Always Valid approach allows us to gather most of the validations for an entity in a single place, and thus simplify the relational logic. So, what approach to choose and why? Despite the benefits of the Not Always Valid approach provides, I strongly recommend you adhere to the Always Valid approach.

- Prefer the "Always Valid" approach because :
  - Removes temporal coupling
  - Helps with DRY
  - Classes maintain their invariants

There are two reasons for that. First of all, it removes temporal coupling. With the opposite technique, you must always remember to call the isValid method before persisting an entity to the database, or before executing some business critical operation. This often ends up to be an error prone way to build a domain model. Secondly, the Always Valid approach helps with the don't repeat yourself principle. In other words, it helps eliminate duplications which inevitably take place with the Not Always valid approach, because of the necessity to validate domain entities multiple times during a single business operation. Overall, it is better to adhere to the guideline stating that all domain entities and value objects should always reside in a valid state and maintain their invariants during the full length of their lifetime. A violation of any invariant in the domain model should signalize a bug and lead to a failure in order to protect the persistent state. This principle is often referred to as fail-fast and is one of the most important principles of software development. So, if all domain classes reside in the valid state, where exactly should one perform validations? Where should we check that an item can be added to a cargo?

- Validations should be at the domain layer boundaries

```
String err = snackMachine.canBuySnack(position);
if(err != string.isEmpty()){
showError(error);
return;
}
snackMachine.BuySnack(position);
```

The best place to perform such validations is the boundary of the domain layer in the Application Services. You saw this technique in our project. Whenever we needed to validate whether a snack could be bought from a snack machine or a sum of money could be taken from an ATM, we performed validations in the controller first, and only after that performed the corresponding operation upon the domain entities. This way we ensured all classes in our domain model always reside in a valid state. Otherwise, our domain classes throw exceptions, which lead to application crash.

Factories

- Create domain entities

- Complex creation logic
- Helps simplify entities
- Don't use factories in case the creation logic is simple

One of the DDD concepts we didn't use in our sample application is factory. Factory is not a DDD notion per say, it was first described by the Gang of Four in the Design Patterns book, but it's still worth discussing. A factory is a class, which is responsible for creation of domain entities. Sometimes creating an entity requires a lot of work in a sense that you need to retrieve some information from different places and combine different pieces of it together in a certain way. In this case, it would be unwise to commission this responsibility to the entity itself, because construction of an entity has nothing to do with exploiting it after that. Think about it this way. A car engine is a complex device, but it's not responsible for self-construction. That is what engine factories are for. Designing an engine which can build itself is in theory a feasible task, but such a device would most likely be too expensive and unstable compared to a classic car engine. The same reasoning is applicable to domain entities. If the logic for creating them is complex, it is better to extract this responsibility to a separate factory class. That would help keep the entity simple and thus more maintainable. Just as repositories, factories create whole aggregates, not just separate entities in it. At the same time, don't add a separate factory in case the initialization logic is simple enough. Class constructors would be a better option in such a situation. You saw that in our domain model, we didn't introduce any factories. That's because there wasn't any complex business logic associated to the creation of our entities.

Domain Services vs. Application Services

- Domain Services :
  - Don't have state
  - Contain domain logic
  - Possess knowledge that doesn't belong to entities and value objects

Another important DDD concept we didn't discuss yet is Domain Services. A Domain Service is a class which doesn't have any state associated with it and which contains some domain logic. The best way to think about Domain Services is to view them as containers for the knowledge which doesn't belong to any entity or value object, but is still essential for your domain. It might happen that an operation is related to some entity, but representing it as a method in that entity wouldn't make much sense. In this case, it is probably a good idea to delegate this operation to a domain service. An example here would be a car service. We don't entrust a responsibility to maintain a vehicle to the vehicle itself. It's just not the way it works in the real world. A better decision would be to introduce a separate domain service responsible for that operation. A question which often arises when people start thinking of Domain Services is how they differ from Application Services.

- Domain Service:
    - Inside of the domain layer
    - Contains domain logic
    - Doesn't communicate with the outside world
- Application Service:
    - Outside of the domain layer
    - Doesn't contain domain logic
    - Communicates with the outside world

The difference here is that an Application Service resides outside of the domain layer, whereas a Domain Service is inside of it. It means that Application Services are in charge of communicating with the outside world and shouldn't contain any domain logic. What they should do instead is delegate the execution to the domain classes, such as entities, repositories, and Domain Services. Domain Services, on the other hand, do contain domain knowledge and shouldn't communicate with the classes outside of the domain layer, the two innermost layers in the onion architecture. We didn't have any Domain Services in our project, but at some point, we could. For example, if we had a requirement to distribute a given amount of products evenly among several snack machines, that would be a task for a Domain Service, because it is a domain-related operation and it doesn't fit the responsibilities of any existing entity in our domain.

Anemic Domain Model Anti-pattern

There are several pitfalls programmers starting with DDD may run into, and it's important to know about them. One of such pitfalls is anemic domain model. If you try to follow DDD principles, then you are probably not subjected to this anti-pattern, but it's still worthwhile to know about it. Anemic domain model stands for separating data and methods working on that data to separate classes. It usually means that entities in such models contain only data and all domain logic is extracted to Domain Services. In our application, for example, anemic domain model would look like this.

```
public class SnackMachine extends AggregateRoot{
public Money moneyInside;
public decimal moneyInTransaction{ get; set;
}
public List<Slot> slots;
}
public class SnackMachineService{
public void buySnack(SnackMachine snackMachine, int position) {}
public void loadSnacks(SnackMachine snackMachine, int position, SnackPile snackPile) {}
public void loadMoney(SnackMachine snackMachine, Money money) {}
}
```

- Poor encapsulation

You can see the snack machine entity contains only data, moneyInside, moneyInTransaction,

259

and the collection of slots. All operations up on the snack machine are delegated to the snack machine domain service. In object-oriented programming languages, introducing an anemic domain model is generally a bad idea, because it hinders application of many OPD design patterns and best practices. The most important drawback here is that it often leads to poor encapsulation. Note that the properties in the snack machine entities are all public. That's no coincidence. The only way to enable separation of data and logic into different classes is to expose the internal structure of domain entities and thus break their encapsulation. Such code is much harder to maintain, because its invariants can be easily broken.

Fat Entities Anti-pattern

- Too much logic in entities
- Entities with unnatural responsibilities
- Look up date in external sources
- Communicate with external layers

Another anti-pattern I'd like to mention is fat entities. This anti-pattern resides on the other part of the spectrum of bad design decisions comparing to anemic domain model, and basically stands for putting too much logic to entities. There is a fine balance between anemic domain model and fat entities, and it's sometimes hard to find it. So, how do you know that you put too much logic to your entities? One of the clues is that your entities start having responsibilities that seem unnatural to them. For example, in our sample application, we could commission the duty to update the balance of the head office to the ATM entity. Such responsibility doesn't make a lot of sense in our domain, because ATMs don't actually update the balance of our office. Nevertheless, we could do that and that would be a sign of the ATM entity getting too fat. Another symptom of this anti-pattern is when domain entities start looking up data in the database or communicating with outer layers of the onion architecture. In other words, when we break isolation and allow the innermost layer depends on the classes from outer layers. To avoid falling into the trap of fat entities, you need to make sure your domain model is properly isolated, and all entities' responsibilities make sense from the domain point of view.

Repository Anti-patterns

There also is a quite common anti-pattern involving the repositories. It regards to the way a repository initializes domain entities that are returned in different methods. Let's elaborate on that. Let's say, for example, that we have three scenarios, each of which requires a different set of data from snack machines.

```
public class SnackMachineRepository extends
Repository{
        public List<SnackMachine> getAll(){
                /* Return a list of fully
        initialized machines */
        }
```

```
public List<SnackMachine>
getAllWithoutSlots(){
        /* Return a list of machines
without slots */
}
public List<SnackMachine>
getOnlyIds(){
        /* Return a list of machines with
only identifiers */
}
}
```

- Partially initialized entities

The first one needs all data associated with snack machines in the database. So, we create a method in our repository, like this. Another scenario doesn't need slots from the database, so we decide to create a separate method, which also returns all snack machines from the database, but doesn't fetch slots attached to them. This would allow us to improve the performance of fetch operation, because we reduce the amount of data we retrieve from the database. And finally, the third scenario requires only the machine's identifiers, so we add a third method which also returns a list of snack machines, but fills only the ID property of them. All other fields remain empty. This allows us to improve the database select query even further. This technique leaves us with three methods. Each of them is perfectly justified from the performance point of view, because each of them returns only the data that is required in one particular case. The problem with this approach, however, is that these two methods return partially initialized entities. And with partially initialized properties, we cannot ensure validity of the entities and thus cannot adhere to the Always Valid approach we discussed previously. In our case, snack machines should always contain exactly three slots, and by not returning them along with the machines, we violate this business rule. Partial initialization leads to inability to maintain invariants of the entities and thus should be avoided. If your repository returns a domain entity, make sure it is fully initialized, meaning that all its properties are filled out. But what should we do in case we really need the performance benefits partial initialization provides? The solution here is not to use domain entities as returning objects in such situations. So in this case, we can keep the three methods, but use other data structures instead of snack machine entities. For the method that returns all machine properties except slots, we can use data transfer objects and put this data there. For the third method, we can employ the long type and return IDs as is without wrapping them into a separate class. Not only does this approach solve the problem with the validity of snack machines, but it also makes explicit what data the repository methods return. This Dto class doesn't contain a slot collection, so we won't be able to accidentally access it. When we'll be processing the DTO on the client side, the compiler would notify us about that.

Mechanical Approach to DDD

The last anti-pattern I'd like to talk about is mechanical approach to domain-driven design. I've seen several times how programmers start treating their domain mechanically. Whenever they defined a new concept in the domain model, they automatically created several classes for it, a class for the concept itself, a repository, a factory, and a domain service. They did that even if there was no need for those classes. Don't do that. Not only does such approach violate the YAGNI principle, it also greatly diminishes the benefits of domain-driven design. Domain modeling is not something we can automate or commission to external tools. The act of modeling is closely related to learning. When we build our domain model, we first and foremost learn the domain we are working in. The code is an artifact of that learning process. Mechanical approach to building the model, as well as mechanical approach to learning doesn't do any good. The only way to perform that is to do it thoughtfully. It also means that such tools as code generation and scaffolding don't help with this process, either. If you find yourself relying on a code generation tool for building your domain model, you are most likely falling into the trap of mechanical approach to domain-driven design.

Further Enhancements

Let's overview our application and see what further enhancements it can potentially take in the future. This is the map of the bounded contexts we ended up with in the previous module.

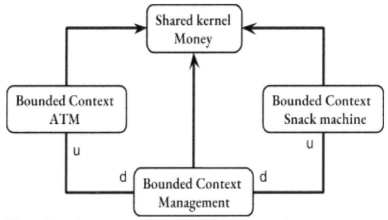

Note that they are rather small in a sense that they contain few entities each. In the real world application, they would probably be bigger, because a typical application usually has much more requirements than we covered during this course. One of such requirements could be constructing a snack machine with different parameters, such as various numbers of slots, products, specialization, and so on. And that can be potentially be the direction in which the development will move further on. This additional functionality would belong to the snack machine bounded context. Also, we would probably need some kind of product supply for the snack machines our company owns in order to be able to refill them in a timely manner. This would belong to another bounded context, product supply, and it would contain its own version of the product entity, because the perspective from which the two bounded contexts view this entity differs, despite the fact these classes will represent the same physical product. For the ATM bounded context, we will probably need a collection service, which would reveal cash in them. That would also be an additional bounded context with its own representation of ATMs.

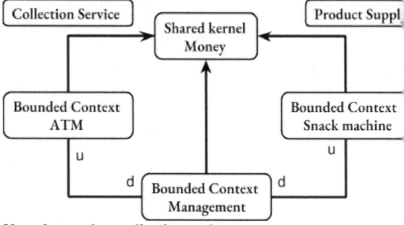

Note that as the application evolves, we can change the boundaries of the bounded contexts. That's perfectly fine as long as we state those changes explicitly in the context map. We can also change the type of physical isolation we employ for them. As the bounded contexts we work on grow, we can extract them into separate microservices and draw them as independent applications.

Module Summary

- **Factories**
- **Domain Services vs Application Services**
- **Always Valid vs Not Always Valid approaches**
- **Anemic domain model**
- **Fat entities**
- **Repository anti-patterns**
- **Mechanical approach to DDD**
- **Further enhancements**

In this module, we discussed several DDD concepts we didn't touch upon in the previous modules. We talked about factories, classes that should be used to remove responsibility to properly initialize domain entities from the entities themselves. It's a good practice to employ that pattern in case the initialization logic gets too complex. We looked at the notion of Domain Services and how it differs from Application Services. The main difference here is that Domain Services reside inside the main layer, and thus contain domain knowledge, whereas Application Services coordinate the work between the domain layer and the outer world. We discussed the dichotomy of Always Valid versus Not Always Valid approaches to entities and value objects. It's a good practice to adhere to the Always Valid way of working with domain objects, and don't allow them to break the invariants. That would help eliminate duplications in code and adhere to the fail-fast principle. We talked about two anti-patterns that reside on the opposite side of the spectrum, anemic domain model and fat entities. Don't run two extremes, and always keep balance between the two. We also talked about a common anti-pattern, which sometimes arises when it comes to working with repositories. Make sure that every repository method return a domain entity fully initializes that entity. If you need some partial data from you database, use data transfer objects instead. We discussed mechanical approach to domain-driven design. Domain modeling is one of the most important parts of software development. Make sure you treat it accordingly and pay close attention to that process. Finally, we talked about further enhancements our sample application can potentially take in the future.

Book Summary

- Full application from scratch
- Domain modeling
- DDD concepts in practice
- Spring Boot
- Database and ORM
- Unit testing
- MVC

We've made great progress in this book. We've built a small, but fairly complex application from the very beginning using domain-driven design principles. You saw how DDD helps us focus on the essential parts of the software, its domain model, and how it allows us to simplify this model and thus keep it maintainable in the long run. You learned the differences between entities and value objects, how to keep the model isolated in the face of working with a relational database, and an ORM, how to work with aggregates, repositories, bounded contexts, and domain events. You also saw how DDD plays with unit testing and MVC design pattern. Thank you.

www.ingramcontent.com/pod-product-compliance
Lightning Source LLC
LaVergne TN
LVHW051223050326
832903LV00028B/2237